DICTIONARY
NEMONIK THINKING

Second Edition

Nemoniks >>> Keywords
Keywords >>> Nemoniks

Dr. Auke Schade

nemonik-thinking.org

Copyright

Second Edition
Published 1 July 2016
@ nemonik-thinking.org
ISBN 978-0-473-36459-5

Abstract

Nemonik thinking mobilizes your hidden genius, accelerates your thinking, improves your memory, reveals opportunities and threats, creates questions and ideas, and reduces your stress levels. Nemonik thinking divides the mind into 17 nemonik regions. Those regions defragment information, which facilitates the storage, maintenance, recall, and processing of associated information from memory. However, the boundaries of those nemonik regions are fuzzy. Therefore, the aim of this dictionary is to differentiate them by providing keywords for each nemonik concept. The first part of this dictionary translates nemonik concepts into common keywords (e.g. *advance* into attack, bypass, etc.). In contrast, the second part translates common keywords into nemonik concepts (e.g. attack, bypass, etc. into *advance*). This dictionary shows that the complexity of conventional thinking comprises thousands of keywords that can be simplified to 17 nemoniks. This reduction will increase the speed of your thinking. To become skilled in nemonik thinking, it is recommended to study—*Think Smarter with Nemonik Thinking (Schade, 2016).*

Dr Auke Schade

My life started during the devastation of World War II. As a teenager, I worked as a carpenter and studied building engineering at night school. During the seventies, I became a financial manager for a multinational corporation, ran my own business, and studied economics in my spare time. My interest in the psychology of management extended to the interaction between the mind, body, and reality. In 1980, I immigrated to New Zealand where I obtained a doctorate in psychology from the University of Auckland. My mission is to make people the smartest thinkers they can be, which has led me to the development of nemonik thinking.[i]

Reality shows that humanity's way of thinking is failing dramatically. As a result, the next generation is facing overpopulation, dwindling resources, nuclear warfare, industrial pollution, climate change, etc. Therefore, they have to become the best thinkers they can be.

Download free eBooks and videos
@ nemonik-thinking.org

---

i Appendix: Nemonik Thinking.

Notes

CONTENTS

Free eBooks and videos
@ nemonik-thinking.org

DIAGRAM NEMONIK THINKING

Nemonik thinking
    Mind
        Conscious
            Rational thinking
                OBJECTIVE-1
                COLLECTIVE-2
        Subconscious
            Affectorial thinking
                CREATIVE-3
                REACTIVE-4
    Reality
            Space
                ADVANCE-5
                STAY-6
                RETREAT-7
            Matter
                ACCUMULATE-8
                PRESERVE-9
                DISPOSE-10
            Time
                ACT-11
                WAIT-12
                PREPARE-13
    Interaction
            Perception
                ACCEPT-14
                REJECT-15
            Projection
                REVEAL-16
                CONCEAL-17

Notes

PART-I: NEMONIKS TO KEYWORDS

ACCEPT

Accept—perceptual nemonik that prompts the mind to accept the incoming information as a true description of the sensory reality. Path > nemonik thinking / interaction / perception / **accept**

Accept—abide
Accept—accede
Accept—accept
Accept—accord
Accept—accustom
Accept—acquiesce
Accept—adjust
Accept—admit
Accept—adore
Accept—advocate
Accept—affection
Accept—agreement
Accept—align
Accept—allow
Accept—amiable
Accept—appease
Accept—appreciate
Accept—approve
Accept—authenticate
Accept—authorize
Accept—bamboozled
Accept—benevolent
Accept—betrayed
Accept—careless
Accept—cheated
Accept—choice
Accept—communicate
Accept—compatible
Accept—comply
Accept—compromise

Accept—concede
Accept—conciliate
Accept—concur
Accept—confirm
Accept—confirmation
Accept—conform
Accept—conned
Accept—consent
Accept—conversation
Accept—convinced
Accept—data
Accept—deceived
Accept—defrauded
Accept—deluded
Accept—details
Accept—devote
Accept—diagnose
Accept—docile
Accept—double-crossed
Accept—duped
Accept—dynamic
Accept—easy to fool
Accept—embrace
Accept—empathy
Accept—endorse
Accept—ensnared
Accept—entangled
Accept—entrapped
Accept—facilitate
Accept—facts
Accept—fatigued
Accept—fiddled
Accept—figures
Accept—fleeced
Accept—flexible
Accept—follow
Accept—fooled

Accept—friends
Accept—generous
Accept—go-ahead
Accept—grant
Accept—gullible
Accept—hallucinated
Accept—hustled
Accept—imaginary
Accept—impassive
Accept—indulgent
Accept—inexperienced
Accept—innocent
Accept—interaction
Accept—kind
Accept—language
Accept—lax
Accept—lured
Accept—malleable
Accept—mediate
Accept—misled
Accept—moderate
Accept—mollify
Accept—naive
Accept—nemonik thinking
Accept—news media
Accept—non-assertive
Accept—non-critical
Accept—non-judgmental
Accept—numbers
Accept—obey
Accept—pacify
Accept—peace
Accept—Perception
Accept—permit
Accept—placate
Accept—pliable
Accept—promise

Accept—ratify
Accept—recognition
Accept—recommend
Accept—reconcile
Accept—resolve
Accept—rip off
Accept—risk taking
Accept—self-deception
Accept—selfless
Accept—settle
Accept—sign
Accept—snared
Accept—solidarity
Accept—soothe
Accept—spineless
Accept—submissive
Accept—succumb
Accept—support
Accept—surrender
Accept—swindled
Accept—sympathetic
Accept—tolerate
Accept—trapped
Accept—treaty
Accept—tricked
Accept—truce
Accept—trust
Accept—uncritical
Accept—unify
Accept—unquestioning
Accept—unselfish
Accept—unsuspecting
Accept—unworried
Accept—willing
Accept—yielding

ACCUMULATE

Accumulate—material nemonik that prompts the mind to increase the amount of matter that is under control. Path > nemonik thinking / reality / matter / **accumulate**

Accumulate—abundance
Accumulate—accrue
Accumulate—accumulate
Accumulate—acquire
Accumulate—add
Accumulate—affluence
Accumulate—aggressive
Accumulate—amass
Accumulate—animals
Accumulate—annex
Accumulate—antagonize
Accumulate—assemble
Accumulate—assets
Accumulate—attain
Accumulate—augment
Accumulate—borrow
Accumulate—breed
Accumulate—build
Accumulate—bully
Accumulate—buy
Accumulate—capital
Accumulate—capture
Accumulate—cash
Accumulate—catch
Accumulate—chattels
Accumulate—claim
Accumulate—combine
Accumulate—conquer
Accumulate—construct
Accumulate—copious
Accumulate—cultivate

Accumulate—data
Accumulate—develop
Accumulate—earn
Accumulate—educate
Accumulate—employ
Accumulate—energy
Accumulate—enhance
Accumulate—enlarge
Accumulate—enrich
Accumulate—equipment
Accumulate—excess
Accumulate—expand
Accumulate—extend
Accumulate—extravagant
Accumulate—facts
Accumulate—figures
Accumulate—fluid
Accumulate—forage
Accumulate—force
Accumulate—fortune
Accumulate—foster
Accumulate—friends
Accumulate—funds
Accumulate—gain
Accumulate—gas
Accumulate—gather
Accumulate—goods
Accumulate—grab
Accumulate—grasp
Accumulate—greed
Accumulate—grow
Accumulate—hire
Accumulate—hoard
Accumulate—hunt
Accumulate—incorporate
Accumulate—increase
Accumulate—information

Accumulate—invest
Accumulate—join
Accumulate—knowledge
Accumulate—lavish
Accumulate—learn
Accumulate—lease
Accumulate—logic
Accumulate—luxury
Accumulate—machinery
Accumulate—make
Accumulate—manufacture
Accumulate—material
Accumulate—matter
Accumulate—memorize
Accumulate—merge
Accumulate—minerals
Accumulate—money
Accumulate—nemonik thinking
Accumulate—numbers
Accumulate—nurture
Accumulate—obtain
Accumulate—occupy
Accumulate—opulence
Accumulate—oversupply
Accumulate—overthrow
Accumulate—overwhelm
Accumulate—ownership
Accumulate—people
Accumulate—plants
Accumulate—plenty
Accumulate—positioning
Accumulate—possession
Accumulate—practice
Accumulate—procure
Accumulate—produce
Accumulate—profit
Accumulate—profuse

Accumulate—progress
Accumulate—propagate
Accumulate—property
Accumulate—prosperity
Accumulate—provoke
Accumulate—purchase
Accumulate—raid
Accumulate—raise
Accumulate—raw material
Accumulate—reality
Accumulate—recruit
Accumulate—remember
Accumulate—resources
Accumulate—revenue
Accumulate—rich
Accumulate—rob
Accumulate—robots
Accumulate—seize
Accumulate—snatch
Accumulate—stack
Accumulate—staff
Accumulate—stash
Accumulate—statistics
Accumulate—steal
Accumulate—stingy
Accumulate—stock
Accumulate—study
Accumulate—supplies
Accumulate—support
Accumulate—surplus
Accumulate—take
Accumulate—takeover
Accumulate—threat
Accumulate—tight-fisted
Accumulate—tools
Accumulate—trade
Accumulate—treasure

Accumulate—unite
Accumulate—upgrade
Accumulate—utensils
Accumulate—vehicles
Accumulate—wages
Accumulate—wealth
Accumulate—workforce
Accumulate—yield

ACT

Act—temporal nemonik that prompts the mind to change or move matter in space and time. Path > nemonik thinking / reality / time / **act**

Act—act
Act—aggressive
Act—antagonize
Act—brave
Act—bully
Act—careless
Act—carry out
Act—commitment
Act—courage
Act—daring
Act—decisive
Act—deed
Act—do
Act—dogged
Act—efficient
Act—execute
Act—get
Act—go
Act—go-getter
Act—haste
Act—impatient
Act—impetuous
Act—impulsive
Act—incautious
Act—initiative
Act—interfere
Act—irrefutable
Act—mettle
Act—nemonik thinking
Act—nerve
Act—nip in the bud

Act—opportunism
Act—panic
Act—perform
Act—positioning
Act—preclude
Act—premature
Act—prevent
Act—proactive
Act—provoke
Act—rash
Act—reality
Act—reckless
Act—reflex
Act—resolute
Act—response
Act—retort
Act—risk taking
Act—roused
Act—speed
Act—stance
Act—stanch
Act—steadfast
Act—steady
Act—strike
Act—sure
Act—tackle
Act—threat
Act—time
Act—unbending
Act—unwavering
Act—valour

ADVANCE

Advance—spatial nemonik that prompts the mind to decrease the distance to the goal. Path > nemonik thinking / reality / space / **advance**

Advance—advance
Advance—aggressive
Advance—antagonize
Advance—assault
Advance—attack
Advance—break into
Advance—bully
Advance—bypass
Advance—charge
Advance—chase
Advance—claim
Advance—conquer
Advance—cut off
Advance—develop
Advance—dialectic
Advance—discover
Advance—expand
Advance—explore
Advance—extend
Advance—extrapolate
Advance—force
Advance—forge ahead
Advance—forward
Advance—go into
Advance—headway
Advance—hunt
Advance—incursion
Advance—infiltrate
Advance—infringe
Advance—initiative
Advance—intercept

Advance—intrude
Advance—invade
Advance—knowledge
Advance—logic
Advance—momentum
Advance—move ahead
Advance—nemonik thinking
Advance—offensive
Advance—outflank
Advance—outrun
Advance—overrun
Advance—overthrow
Advance—overwhelm
Advance—penetrate
Advance—perforate
Advance—pierce
Advance—pioneer
Advance—plunge
Advance—positioning
Advance—pounce
Advance—prod
Advance—progress
Advance—promote
Advance—propagate
Advance—provoke
Advance—puncture
Advance—pursue
Advance—push
Advance—raid
Advance—reality
Advance—rush
Advance—search
Advance—seize
Advance—shunt
Advance—space
Advance—spearhead
Advance—speed

27

Advance—storm
Advance—strike
Advance—supply lines
Advance—surpass
Advance—surprise
Advance—surround
Advance—swoop
Advance—threat
Advance—thrust
Advance—unexpected
Advance—unknown territory
Advance—vanguard

AFFECTERS

Affecters—mental signals that are generated by subconscious affectorial thinking, which influence the conscious without explaining the underlying subconscious processes. Affecters do not rely on conscious reasoning or facts, and therefore, they are by definition non-rational and illogical. Path > nemonik thinking / mind / subconscious / affectorial thinking / affecters

affecters—beliefs
affecters—desires
affecters—discoveries
affecters—emotions
affecters—fantasies
affecters—habits
affecters—heuristics
affecters—ideas
affecters—impulses
affecters—innovations
affecters—insights,
affecters—inspirations
affecters—intuitions
affecters—inventions
affecters—mental signals
affecters—novelties
affecters—reactions
affecters—reflexes
affecters—routines
affecters—skills

AFFECTORIAL THINKING

Affectorial thinking—subconscious part of nemonik thinking that deals with the unpredictable chaos of reality by generating affecters that influence the conscious. Path > nemonik thinking / mind / subconscious / **affectorial thinking**

affectorial thinking—alpha brainwaves
affectorial thinking—alpha-state
affectorial thinking—calm
affectorial thinking—catnap
affectorial thinking—character
affectorial thinking—charisma
affectorial thinking—confidence
affectorial thinking—Creative
affectorial thinking—doze
affectorial thinking—efficient
affectorial thinking—empty mind
affectorial thinking—illogical
affectorial thinking—individual
affectorial thinking—insight
affectorial thinking—irrational
affectorial thinking—meditation
affectorial thinking—mental prompts
affectorial thinking—mental signals
affectorial thinking—mind
affectorial thinking—mind management
affectorial thinking—napping
affectorial thinking—nemonik thinking
affectorial thinking—organize
affectorial thinking—personal
affectorial thinking—prompt
affectorial thinking—Reactive
affectorial thinking—relax
affectorial thinking—rest
affectorial thinking—semiconscious dominance
affectorial thinking—signals

affectorial thinking—silent mind
affectorial thinking—sleep
affectorial thinking—slumber
affectorial thinking—subconscious
affectorial thinking—subjective
affectorial thinking—suggestibility
affectorial thinking—time-out
affectorial thinking—train
affectorial thinking—twilight state
affectorial thinking—uncritical
affectorial thinking—unknown
affectorial thinking—unplanned
affectorial thinking—unpredictable
affectorial thinking—unproven
affectorial thinking—unreasonable
affectorial thinking—unsubstantiated
affectorial thinking—unsystematic
affectorial thinking—wisdom
affectorial thinking—zone

COLLECTIVE

Collective mindmode—way of rational thinking that generates artificial rules, which determine the rights and obliga-
tions of individuals within a collective and makes their behaviours predictable. Collective refers to an organized
group of people with a common goal such as a family,
business, tribe, nation, or the entire human race. Path >
nemonik thinking / mind / conscious / rational thinking /
collective

Collective—accurate
Collective—accuse
Collective—adjust
Collective—administration
Collective—aggression
Collective—agreement
Collective—aid
Collective—alert
Collective—alliance
Collective—alterable
Collective—amalgamate
Collective—amendable
Collective—Analects
Collective—analyses
Collective—anticipate
Collective—antitheses
Collective—arbitrary
Collective—argument
Collective—Aristotle
Collective—arrangement
Collective—artificial
Collective—artificial intelligence
Collective—assemble
Collective—assistance
Collective—associate
Collective—attention

Collective—attorney
Collective—audience
Collective—authority
Collective—awake
Collective—aware
Collective—barrister
Collective—behaviour
Collective—belonging
Collective—bluff
Collective—body language
Collective—body posture
Collective—books
Collective—brainwashing
Collective—bureaucracy
Collective—business
Collective—calculating
Collective—callousness
Collective—camaraderie
Collective—care
Collective—categories
Collective—causation
Collective—cause
Collective—cause-effect
Collective—certain
Collective—chain of command
Collective—changeable
Collective—civil law
Collective—civil service
Collective—claim
Collective—closeness
Collective—club
Collective—coalition
Collective—code of conduct
Collective—coerce
Collective—cognitive
Collective—coherent
Collective—collaborate

Collective—collective
Collective—collective truth
Collective—combine
Collective—commercial law
Collective—common ground
Collective—common law
Collective—commonality
Collective—communal law
Collective—communicate
Collective—community
Collective—companionship
Collective—comprehension
Collective—comradeship
Collective—concentrate
Collective—conclusion
Collective—condition
Collective—confederate
Collective—conflict
Collective—conform
Collective—Confucius
Collective—conscious
Collective—conscious dominance
Collective—consciousness
Collective—consequence
Collective—consider
Collective—consistent
Collective—consortium
Collective—constrain
Collective—contemplate
Collective—contract
Collective—contribution
Collective—control
Collective—conversation
Collective—conviction
Collective—convince
Collective—cooperate
Collective—correct

Collective—corroborate
Collective—countable
Collective—court of law
Collective—criminal
Collective—criminal law
Collective—critical
Collective—customs
Collective—cynical
Collective—data
Collective—deal breakers
Collective—deal makers
Collective—debate
Collective—decision
Collective—decree
Collective—deductive
Collective—deliberate
Collective—demonstrate
Collective—deserter
Collective—details
Collective—deterministic
Collective—diagnose
Collective—dialectic
Collective—disagreement
Collective—disbelieve
Collective—discipline
Collective—discourse
Collective—discriminate
Collective—discussion
Collective—dispassion
Collective—dissent
Collective—distrust
Collective—doctrines
Collective—dogma
Collective—doubt
Collective—drill
Collective—duty
Collective—educate

Collective—efficient
Collective—effort
Collective—emotionless
Collective—enforce
Collective—enquiry
Collective—esprit de corps
Collective—esteem
Collective—ethics
Collective—evaluate
Collective—evidence
Collective—examine
Collective—exchange
Collective—exercise
Collective—expectation
Collective—expert
Collective—face loss
Collective—face saving
Collective—facts
Collective—fairness
Collective—family
Collective—fashionable
Collective—fast
Collective—federation
Collective—figures
Collective—focus
Collective—follow
Collective—force
Collective—forecast
Collective—formal
Collective—formal logic
Collective—fortune
Collective—fraternize
Collective—friends
Collective—funds
Collective—fuse
Collective—gesticulation
Collective—gestures

Collective—give-and-take
Collective—government
Collective—group
Collective—groupthink
Collective—habituation
Collective—healthcare
Collective—hierarchy
Collective—honour
Collective—hostility
Collective—hypothesis
Collective—hypothetical
Collective—if-then arguments
Collective—impartial
Collective—impersonal
Collective—impose
Collective—incorporate
Collective—indoctrinate
Collective—inductive reason
Collective—inequality
Collective—inference
Collective—influence
Collective—infrastructure
Collective—injustice
Collective—innocent
Collective—inquest
Collective—institution
Collective—insurance
Collective—insurgent
Collective—integrate
Collective—internalize
Collective—interpolate
Collective—intimidate
Collective—investigate
Collective—join forces
Collective—joint-venture
Collective—judge
Collective—judgement

Collective—judiciary
Collective—know-how
Collective—knowledge
Collective—language
Collective—Lao Zi
Collective—law and order
Collective—law enforcement
Collective—law of causality
Collective—law-making
Collective—laws
Collective—lawyer
Collective—leader
Collective—leadership
Collective—league
Collective—learn
Collective—least effort
Collective—least resistance
Collective—legalize
Collective—letters
Collective—liaise
Collective—logic
Collective—love
Collective—magistrate
Collective—making rules
Collective—mana
Collective—management
Collective—manipulate
Collective—manmade
Collective—mannerisms
Collective—manufacture
Collective—maximize
Collective—mediate
Collective—mental model
Collective—mental process
Collective—messages
Collective—methodical
Collective—meticulous

Collective—military
Collective—mind
Collective—minimum effort
Collective—mistrust
Collective—modifiable
Collective—money
Collective—morals
Collective—motivate
Collective—mottos
Collective—mutable
Collective—mutiny
Collective—mutual support
Collective—nation
Collective—negative reinforcement
Collective—negotiate
Collective—nemonik accelerator
Collective—nemonik thinking
Collective—network
Collective—nonconforming
Collective—numbers
Collective—obligation
Collective—Ockham's razor
Collective—officials
Collective—opposition
Collective—oppress
Collective—order
Collective—organize
Collective—ostracise
Collective—outcast
Collective—outlaw
Collective—overrule
Collective—overthrow
Collective—overwhelm
Collective—pacify
Collective—pact
Collective—parliament
Collective—partnership

Collective—pattern
Collective—peer pressure
Collective—penalty
Collective—people
Collective—perfection
Collective—persuade
Collective—police
Collective—policies
Collective—politicians
Collective—politics
Collective—positioning
Collective—positive reinforcement
Collective—power
Collective—precise
Collective—predict
Collective—prejudice
Collective—premise
Collective—prerogative
Collective—prestige
Collective—privilege
Collective—probe
Collective—procedures
Collective—proficiency
Collective—programming
Collective—progress
Collective—propaganda
Collective—prosecutor
Collective—protocols
Collective—prove
Collective—public law
Collective—punish
Collective—purge
Collective—question
Collective—quick
Collective—rapid
Collective—ratify
Collective—rational thinking

Collective—reason
Collective—reasonable
Collective—rebel
Collective—reciprocity
Collective—red tape
Collective—regulate
Collective—relationship
Collective—reliable
Collective—representatives
Collective—repress
Collective—reputation
Collective—resentment
Collective—resistance
Collective—respect
Collective—review
Collective—revolt
Collective—reward
Collective—rights
Collective—rules
Collective—ruling
Collective—safety
Collective—sarcastic
Collective—scare
Collective—sceptic
Collective—schematic
Collective—scrutinize
Collective—search
Collective—secrets
Collective—sentence
Collective—settlement
Collective—share
Collective—shelter
Collective—skill
Collective—sociable
Collective—social struggle
Collective—society
Collective—solicitor

Collective—specialist
Collective—speed
Collective—stable
Collective—staff
Collective—stance
Collective—statistics
Collective—status
Collective—status quo
Collective—structure
Collective—subdivide
Collective—submission
Collective—subordinates
Collective—successive approximation
Collective—summarize
Collective—supervise
Collective—support
Collective—suppress
Collective—suspicious
Collective—sway
Collective—swear
Collective—swift
Collective—syndicate
Collective—systematic
Collective—team
Collective—team spirit
Collective—team up
Collective—teamwork
Collective—temporary
Collective—terror
Collective—thesis
Collective—together
Collective—train
Collective—traitor
Collective—treaty
Collective—trial
Collective—tribe
Collective—tribunal

Collective—truth
Collective—tyrannize
Collective—understanding
Collective—unemotional
Collective—unfair
Collective—unify
Collective—unite
Collective—unnatural
Collective—uprising
Collective—utilitarian
Collective—validity
Collective—variables
Collective—verdict
Collective—verify
Collective—vigilant
Collective—villain
Collective—violence
Collective—wakeful
Collective—war
Collective—way of least resistance
Collective—written

CONCEAL

Conceal—projectional nemonik that prompts the mind to project false information to the sensory reality. Path > nemonik thinking / interaction / projection / **conceal**

Conceal—aggressive
Conceal—ambush
Conceal—appearance
Conceal—avoid
Conceal—bamboozle
Conceal—betray
Conceal—blind-sight
Conceal—calculating
Conceal—callousness
Conceal—camouflage
Conceal—careful
Conceal—censor
Conceal—cheat
Conceal—choice
Conceal—cloak
Conceal—communicate
Conceal—conceal
Conceal—concoct
Conceal—confuse
Conceal—conversation
Conceal—corrupt
Conceal—cover-up
Conceal—data
Conceal—deceive
Conceal—details
Conceal—disguise
Conceal—dishonest
Conceal—disinform
Conceal—disloyal
Conceal—distrust
Conceal—double-deal

Conceal—doubt
Conceal—duplicity
Conceal—ensnare
Conceal—entice
Conceal—entrap
Conceal—evade
Conceal—fabricate
Conceal—facts
Conceal—feign
Conceal—figures
Conceal—fraud
Conceal—goad
Conceal—half-truth
Conceal—hidden
Conceal—hide
Conceal—hoax
Conceal—hoodwink
Conceal—influence
Conceal—information
Conceal—insincere
Conceal—interaction
Conceal—lie
Conceal—lure
Conceal—make-believe
Conceal—manipulate
Conceal—mask
Conceal—misinform
Conceal—mislead
Conceal—misrepresent
Conceal—mistrust
Conceal—nemonik thinking
Conceal—non-assertive
Conceal—numbers
Conceal—obscure
Conceal—obstruct
Conceal—overt
Conceal—paranoid

Conceal—persistent
Conceal—pretend
Conceal—projection
Conceal—scheme
Conceal—secrets
Conceal—setup
Conceal—sham
Conceal—smokescreen
Conceal—snare
Conceal—spin
Conceal—surprise
Conceal—sway
Conceal—tact
Conceal—tempt
Conceal—threat
Conceal—trap
Conceal—trick
Conceal—undependable
Conceal—unfaithful
Conceal—unreliable
Conceal—untrustworthy
Conceal—untruthful
Conceal—white lie
Conceal—win-lose

CONSCIOUS

Conscious—small part of the mind that is only active when that person is fully awake. Antonym—Subconscious. Path > nemonik thinking / mind / **conscious**

conscious—attention
conscious—awake
conscious—aware
conscious—cognizant
conscious—Collective
conscious—concentrate
conscious—conscious dominance
conscious—consider
conscious—control
conscious—deliberate
conscious—effort
conscious—exercise
conscious—focus
conscious—know
conscious—learn
conscious—manifest
conscious—mental state
conscious—mind
conscious—nemonik accelerator
conscious—nemonik thinking
conscious—Objective
conscious—organize
conscious—rational thinking
conscious—resolution
conscious—roused
conscious—self-assurance
conscious—self-control
conscious—self-discipline
conscious—train
conscious—unemotional
conscious—vigilant

conscious—wakeful
conscious—watchful
conscious—watching
conscious—willpower

CONVENTIONAL THINKING

Conventional thinking—incomplete and unsystematic way of thinking that maximizes the probability of winning by applying a corrupted way of rational thinking propagated by the educational system.

conventional thinking—aggression
conventional thinking—answering
conventional thinking—climate change
conventional thinking—competitions
conventional thinking—conflict oriented
conventional thinking—convergent thinking
conventional thinking—corrupted
conventional thinking—creative thinking
conventional thinking—critical thinking
conventional thinking—criticizing
conventional thinking—deductive thinking
conventional thinking—default
conventional thinking—defeating
conventional thinking—detached
conventional thinking—divergent thinking
conventional thinking—domestic pollution
conventional thinking—dwindling resources
conventional thinking—educated
conventional thinking—educational system
conventional thinking—emotional thinking
conventional thinking—failing
conventional thinking—ill-defined
conventional thinking—incomplete
conventional thinking—inductive thinking
conventional thinking—industrial pollution
conventional thinking—intuitive thinking
conventional thinking—lateral thinking
conventional thinking—linear thinking
conventional thinking—logical thinking
conventional thinking—loose collection

conventional thinking—opponents
conventional thinking—overpopulation
conventional thinking—pollution
conventional thinking—poorly understood
conventional thinking—rational thinking
conventional thinking—rationalizing
conventional thinking—reason
conventional thinking—righteous
conventional thinking—SCARRED
conventional thinking—scientific thinking
conventional thinking—static thinking
conventional thinking—strategical thinking
conventional thinking—tactical thinking
conventional thinking—unsystematic
conventional thinking—vertical thinking
conventional thinking—war
conventional thinking—win-lose strategies
conventional thinking—winning

CREATIVE

Creative mindmode—way of affectorial thinking that deals with the unknown or inexperienced aspects of reality by generating creative affecters. Path > nemonik thinking / mind / subconscious / affectorial thinking / **creative**

Creative—Advance
Creative—affecters
Creative—affectorial thinking
Creative—alpha brainwaves
Creative—alpha-state
Creative—alternatives
Creative—anticipate
Creative—artistic
Creative—behaviour
Creative—biofeedback
Creative—brainstorming
Creative—break
Creative—breather
Creative—bright
Creative—brilliant
Creative—calm
Creative—catnap
Creative—chaos
Creative—cognitive
Creative—conception
Creative—confidence
Creative—creative
Creative—creative affecter
Creative—creative mindmode
Creative—de Bono
Creative—design
Creative—develop
Creative—different
Creative—discover
Creative—disorder (chaos)

Creative—divergent
Creative—doze
Creative—dynamic
Creative—eccentric
Creative—effortless
Creative—empty mind
Creative—evolve
Creative—exceptional
Creative—expand
Creative—explore
Creative—extend
Creative—extrapolate
Creative—fantasy
Creative—fiction
Creative—free association
Creative—generate
Creative—genius
Creative—gestation
Creative—gifted
Creative—ground-breaking
Creative—grow
Creative—Guilford
Creative—hatching
Creative—heretical
Creative—hidden
Creative—hypnosis
Creative—idea
Creative—illogical
Creative—imagination
Creative—inaccessible
Creative—inactive
Creative—inception
Creative—incubation
Creative—inexperience
Creative—ingenious
Creative—innovation
Creative—inspiration

Creative—inspire
Creative—invention
Creative—irrational
Creative—lateral thinking
Creative—meditation
Creative—mental model
Creative—mental process
Creative—mind
Creative—multiple solutions
Creative—napping
Creative—nemonik accelerator
Creative—nemonik thinking
Creative—nemoniks
Creative—new
Creative—non-critical
Creative—non-judgmental
Creative—notion
Creative—novel
Creative—oblivious
Creative—obscure
Creative—opportunity
Creative—original
Creative—peaceful
Creative—pioneer
Creative—progress
Creative—randomization
Creative—realization
Creative—reformulate
Creative—relax
Creative—rest
Creative—search
Creative—semiconscious
Creative—semiconscious dominance
Creative—silent mind
Creative—sleep
Creative—slumber
Creative—spearhead

Creative—state-of-the-art
Creative—strange
Creative—subconscious
Creative—subjective
Creative—surprising
Creative—talent
Creative—thesis
Creative—time-out
Creative—trailblazer
Creative—train
Creative—tranquillity
Creative—turmoil
Creative—twilight state
Creative—unaware
Creative—unconventional
Creative—uncover
Creative—uncritical
Creative—unexpected
Creative—unfamiliar
Creative—unique
Creative—unknown
Creative—unorthodox
Creative—unplanned
Creative—unpredictable
Creative—unproven
Creative—unreasonable
Creative—unsubstantiated
Creative—unsystematic
Creative—untraditional
Creative—unusual
Creative—unwind
Creative—visionary
Creative—zone

DISPOSE

Dispose—material nemonik that prompts the mind to decrease the amount matter that is under control. Path > nemonik thinking / reality / matter / **dispose**

Dispose—abandon
Dispose—animals
Dispose—annihilate
Dispose—assassinate
Dispose—assets
Dispose—ban
Dispose—burn
Dispose—capital
Dispose—cash
Dispose—cast off
Dispose—chattels
Dispose—clear
Dispose—cull
Dispose—cut loss
Dispose—data
Dispose—delete
Dispose—demolish
Dispose—deprivation
Dispose—destroy
Dispose—detach
Dispose—diminish
Dispose—discard
Dispose—discriminate
Dispose—dismantle
Dispose—disperse
Dispose—dispose
Dispose—dissipate
Dispose—distribute
Dispose—divide
Dispose—divorce
Dispose—eject

Dispose—eliminate
Dispose—endow
Dispose—energy
Dispose—equipment
Dispose—eradicate
Dispose—erasure
Dispose—evict
Dispose—exclude
Dispose—exile
Dispose—expulse
Dispose—exterminate
Dispose—extinguish
Dispose—extradite
Dispose—facts
Dispose—famine
Dispose—figures
Dispose—fire
Dispose—fluid
Dispose—force
Dispose—fortune
Dispose—fragmentation
Dispose—friends
Dispose—funds
Dispose—gas
Dispose—generous
Dispose—get rid of
Dispose—give
Dispose—goods
Dispose—grant
Dispose—homicide
Dispose—incompatibility
Dispose—information
Dispose—insufficiency
Dispose—irreconcilable
Dispose—killing
Dispose—knowledge
Dispose—lack

Dispose—lay off
Dispose—lonely
Dispose—lose
Dispose—machinery
Dispose—manslaughter
Dispose—massacre
Dispose—material
Dispose—matter
Dispose—minerals
Dispose—money
Dispose—murder
Dispose—mutiny
Dispose—nemonik thinking
Dispose—non-assertive
Dispose—numbers
Dispose—obliterate
Dispose—obsolete
Dispose—offload
Dispose—ostracise
Dispose—outcast
Dispose—outdated
Dispose—oversupply
Dispose—people
Dispose—plants
Dispose—positioning
Dispose—poverty
Dispose—property
Dispose—punish
Dispose—purge
Dispose—raw material
Dispose—reality
Dispose—recall
Dispose—reduce
Dispose—redundant
Dispose—refuse
Dispose—release
Dispose—remove

Dispose—resign
Dispose—resources
Dispose—revenue
Dispose—robots
Dispose—rubbish
Dispose—sanitize
Dispose—scarcity
Dispose—scorched earth
Dispose—scrap
Dispose—scuttle
Dispose—segmentation
Dispose—send-off
Dispose—separate
Dispose—share
Dispose—shed
Dispose—shortage
Dispose—slash and burn
Dispose—slaughter
Dispose—spendthrift
Dispose—split
Dispose—spread
Dispose—squander
Dispose—staff
Dispose—statistics
Dispose—stock
Dispose—supplies
Dispose—terminate
Dispose—throw away
Dispose—thrust aside
Dispose—tools
Dispose—trash
Dispose—treasure
Dispose—unessential
Dispose—utensils
Dispose—vehicles
Dispose—waste
Dispose—wealth

Dispose—wipe-out
Dispose—workforce

INTERACTION

Interaction—effect of the mind on reality and vice versa.
Path > nemonik thinking / **interaction**

interaction—Accept
interaction—ambiguity
interaction—body language
interaction—body posture
interaction—books
interaction—charisma
interaction—code
interaction—communicate
interaction—Conceal
interaction—conversation
interaction—debate
interaction—delusion
interaction—diplomacy
interaction—discourse
interaction—discussion
interaction—exchange
interaction—eye contact
interaction—facial expression
interaction—fiction
interaction—illusion
interaction—influence
interaction—information
interaction—information management
interaction—interchange
interaction—internet
interaction—language
interaction—letters
interaction—messages
interaction—nemonik thinking
interaction—news media
interaction—non-verbal
interaction—Perception

interaction—projection
interaction—prompt
interaction—question
interaction—Reject
interaction—Reveal
interaction—social media
interaction—validate
interaction—verbal
interaction—words

MATTER

Matter—three-dimensional finite part of reality that features substance, volume, and weight, and occupies and moves through space and time. Path > nemonik thinking / reality / **matter**

matter—Accumulate
matter—animals
matter—assets
matter—body
matter—capital
matter—cash
matter—chattels
matter—circumference
matter—Dispose
matter—energy
matter—equipment
matter—fluid
matter—force
matter—form
matter—fortune
matter—friends
matter—funds
matter—gas
matter—goods
matter—hardness
matter—height
matter—information
matter—inorganic
matter—knowledge
matter—length
matter—logistics
matter—machinery
matter—magnitude
matter—mass
matter—material

matter—minerals
matter—money
matter—nemonik thinking
matter—non-living
matter—organic
matter—people
matter—plants
matter—power
matter—Preserve
matter—profit
matter—property
matter—quality
matter—quantity
matter—raw material
matter—real estate
matter—reality
matter—recruits
matter—resource management
matter—resources
matter—revenue
matter—robots
matter—shape
matter—size
matter—solid
matter—staff
matter—stock
matter—strength
matter—substance
matter—supplies
matter—supply
matter—supply lines
matter—surface
matter—that
matter—thickness
matter—this
matter—three-dimensional
matter—thrust

matter—tools
matter—transform
matter—transport
matter—treasure
matter—utensils
matter—value
matter—vehicles
matter—volume
matter—wealth
matter—weight
matter—what
matter—width
matter—workforce

MEMORY

Memory—self-organising and associative mental process that stores, maintains, and recalls information in order to preserve it across space and time.

memory—associate
memory—brain
memory—brainware
memory—defragmentation
memory—exercise
memory—knowledge
memory—learn
memory—memory pegs
memory—mental checklist
memory—mental network
memory—mental process
memory—mind
memory—mnemonic
memory—neural plasticity
memory—problem solving
memory—prompt
memory—prompt memory
memory—self-organizing
memory—study
memory—train

MIND

Mind—nonmaterial part of a person that comprises the total
of all conscious, subconscious, and semiconscious mental
structures and processes. Path > nemonik thinking / **mind**

mind—affectorial thinking
mind—anticipate
mind—behaviour
mind—being
mind—brain
mind—brainware
mind—character
mind—charisma
mind—choice
mind—closed mind
mind—cognition
mind—Collective
mind—conscious
mind—consciousness
mind—Creative
mind—decision
mind—defragmentation
mind—ego
mind—expect
mind—foreseeable
mind—foresight
mind—hypothetical
mind—I
mind—identity
mind—immaterial
mind—individual
mind—influence
mind—information overload
mind—inner self
mind—insanity
mind—intellect

mind—introspection
mind—learn
mind—me
mind—memory
mind—mental
mind—mental illness
mind—mental layers
mind—mental signals
mind—mental state
mind—mentalism
mind—mentality
mind—mentation
mind—mind management
mind—mindmode
mind—mindware
mind—myself
mind—nemonik accelerator
mind—nemonik thinking
mind—neural plasticity
mind—nonmaterial
mind—Objective
mind—open mind
mind—operating system
mind—option
mind—organize
mind—people
mind—persona
mind—personality
mind—physical
mind—physiological
mind—predict
mind—preference
mind—presumed
mind—problem solving
mind—psychiatry
mind—psychology
mind—rational thinking

mind—Reactive
mind—recall
mind—remember
mind—sanity
mind—self
mind—self-organizing
mind—semiconscious
mind—soul
mind—spirit
mind—subconscious
mind—talent
mind—theoretical construct
mind—thought
mind—traits
mind—unsubstantial
mind—volition
mind—wetware
mind—will
mind—wish

MINDMODE

Mindmode—specific way of thinking that deals with a specific aspect of the external reality. Path > nemonik thinking / mind / **mindmode**

mindmode—Collective
mindmode—Creative
mindmode—Objective
mindmode—Reactive

NEMONIKS

Nemoniks—memorized keywords describing the exhaustive
aspects of the mind, reality, and the interaction of the mind
and reality, which prompt the memory to recall associated
information. Path > nemonik thinking / mind / subconscious / affectorial thinking / **nemoniks.**

nemonik—Accept
nemonik—Accumulate
nemonik—act
nemonik—Advance
nemonik—associate
nemonik—brain
nemonik—brainware
nemonik—cognitive
nemonik—Collective
nemonik—Conceal
nemonik—conscious
nemonik—Creative
nemonik—defragmentation
nemonik—Dispose
nemonik—exhaustive
nemonik—memory pegs
nemonik—mental checklist
nemonik—mental network
nemonik—mental reorganization
nemonik—mental signals
nemonik—mind
nemonik—mind management
nemonik—mindware
nemonik—mnemonic
nemonik—model of the mind
nemonik—neural plasticity
nemonik—Objective
nemonik—operating system
nemonik—prepare

nemonik—Preserve
nemonik—problem solving
nemonik—prompt
nemonik—prompt thinking
nemonik—prompt memory
nemonik—Reactive
nemonik—Reject
nemonik—Retreat
nemonik—Reveal
nemonik—Stay
nemonik—Wait

NEMONIK THINKING

Nemonik thinking—exhaustive and systematic way of thinking that maximizes the probability of success by subjecting seventeen nemoniks to both rational and affectorial thinking.

nemonik thinking—Accept
nemonik thinking—accomplish
nemonik thinking—Accumulate
nemonik thinking—achieve
nemonik thinking—Act
nemonik thinking—Advance
nemonik thinking—affectorial thinking
nemonik thinking—all-inclusive
nemonik thinking—associate
nemonik thinking—automatic process
nemonik thinking—beliefs
nemonik thinking—brain
nemonik thinking—brainware
nemonik thinking—cognitive
nemonik thinking—Collective
nemonik thinking—compassion
nemonik thinking—complete
nemonik thinking—comprehensive
nemonik thinking—Conceal
nemonik thinking—conscious
nemonik thinking—convergent thinking
nemonik thinking—Creative
nemonik thinking—creative thinking
nemonik thinking—critical thinking
nemonik thinking—deductive thinking
nemonik thinking—defragmentation
nemonik thinking—Dispose
nemonik thinking—divergent thinking
nemonik thinking—dynamic
nemonik thinking—dynamic thinking

nemonik thinking—efficient
nemonik thinking—emotional thinking
nemonik thinking—emotions
nemonik thinking—escape
nemonik thinking—every possibility
nemonik thinking—excellence
nemonik thinking—exhaustive
nemonik thinking—goal oriented
nemonik thinking—inductive thinking
nemonik thinking—influence
nemonik thinking—information
nemonik thinking—interaction
nemonik thinking—intuitions
nemonik thinking—intuitive thinking
nemonik thinking—Lao Zi
nemonik thinking—lateral thinking
nemonik thinking—linear thinking
nemonik thinking—logical thinking
nemonik thinking—matter
nemonik thinking—memory
nemonik thinking—memory pegs
nemonik thinking—mental checklist
nemonik thinking—mental network
nemonik thinking—mental process
nemonik thinking—mental reorganization
nemonik thinking—meta-thinking
nemonik thinking—mind
nemonik thinking—mind management
nemonik thinking—mindware
nemonik thinking—mnemonic
nemonik thinking—model of the mind
nemonik thinking—need
nemonik thinking—nemonik accelerator
nemonik thinking—neural plasticity
nemonik thinking—Objective
nemonik thinking—obtain
nemonik thinking—operating system

nemonik thinking—optimize
nemonik thinking—organize
nemonik thinking—people
nemonik thinking—Perception
nemonik thinking—Prepare
nemonik thinking—Preserve
nemonik thinking—problem solving
nemonik thinking—projection
nemonik thinking—prompt
nemonik thinking—prompt memory
nemonik thinking—prompt thinking
nemonik thinking—questioning
nemonik thinking—rational thinking
nemonik thinking—Reactive
nemonik thinking—reality
nemonik thinking—reason
nemonik thinking—Reject
nemonik thinking—Retreat
nemonik thinking—Reveal
nemonik thinking—scientific thinking
nemonik thinking—seek
nemonik thinking—self-organizing
nemonik thinking—semiconscious
nemonik thinking—senses
nemonik thinking—sensory reality
nemonik thinking—space
nemonik thinking—Stay
nemonik thinking—strategical thinking
nemonik thinking—structural thinking
nemonik thinking—subconscious
nemonik thinking—success
nemonik thinking—survival
nemonik thinking—SWOT-analysis
nemonik thinking—systematic
nemonik thinking—systematic thinking
nemonik thinking—tactical thinking
nemonik thinking—teachable

nemonik thinking—time
nemonik thinking—vertical thinking
nemonik thinking—Wait
nemonik thinking—winning
nemonik thinking—win-win strategies
nemonik thinking—wise

OBJECTIVE

Objective mindmode—way of rational thinking that deals
with the natural order of the sensory reality, which can be
described by natural laws and facts that make nature predictable. Path > nemonik thinking / mind / conscious /
rational thinking / **objective**

Objective—accurate
Objective—alert
Objective—analyses
Objective—anticipate
Objective—antitheses
Objective—argument
Objective—Aristotle
Objective—arithmetic
Objective—artificial intelligence
Objective—attention
Objective—awake
Objective—aware
Objective—behaviour
Objective—calculating
Objective—callousness
Objective—categories
Objective—causation
Objective—cause
Objective—cause-effect
Objective—certain
Objective—cognitive
Objective—coherent
Objective—communicate
Objective—comprehension
Objective—compute
Objective—computer
Objective—computer code
Objective—concentrate
Objective—conclusion

Objective—concrete
Objective—conscious
Objective—conscious dominance
Objective—consciousness
Objective—consequence
Objective—consider
Objective—consistent
Objective—constant
Objective—contemplate
Objective—convince
Objective—correct
Objective—countable
Objective—critical
Objective—cynical
Objective—data
Objective—debate
Objective—decision
Objective—deductive
Objective—deliberate
Objective—demonstrate
Objective—detached
Objective—details
Objective—deterministic
Objective—diagnose
Objective—dialectic
Objective—disbelieve
Objective—discourse
Objective—discussion
Objective—dispassion
Objective—dispassionate
Objective—distrust
Objective—doubt
Objective—efficient
Objective—effort
Objective—emotionless
Objective—empirical
Objective—enquiry

Objective—eternal
Objective—eternal truth
Objective—evaluate
Objective—evidence
Objective—exact
Objective—examine
Objective—exercise
Objective—expectation
Objective—experiment
Objective—facts
Objective—figures
Objective—focus
Objective—forecast
Objective—forever
Objective—formal logic
Objective—generalization
Objective—Hegel, F.
Objective—hypothesis
Objective—hypothetical
Objective—if-then arguments
Objective—impartial
Objective—impersonal
Objective—independent
Objective—inductive reason
Objective—industrial revolution
Objective—inference
Objective—informational revolution
Objective—interpolate
Objective—interpret
Objective—investigate
Objective—judgement
Objective—know-how
Objective—knowledge
Objective—Lao Zi
Objective—law of causality
Objective—laws
Objective—learn

Objective—least effort
Objective—least resistance
Objective—level-headed
Objective—literature review
Objective—logic
Objective—mathematics
Objective—maximize
Objective—measurement
Objective—mental model
Objective—mental process
Objective—methodical
Objective—meticulous
Objective—mind
Objective—minimum effort
Objective—mistrust
Objective—natural
Objective—nemonik accelerator
Objective—nemonik thinking
Objective—neutral
Objective—numbers
Objective—objective
Objective—objective truth
Objective—observation
Objective—Ockham's razor
Objective—order
Objective—organize
Objective—pattern
Objective—peer review
Objective—physics
Objective—precise
Objective—predict
Objective—premise
Objective—probe
Objective—progress
Objective—proof
Objective—prove
Objective—question

Objective—random sampling
Objective—rational thinking
Objective—reason
Objective—reasonable
Objective—reliability test
Objective—reliable
Objective—replicable
Objective—result
Objective—review
Objective—samples
Objective—sceptic
Objective—schematic
Objective—science
Objective—scientific truth
Objective—scrutinize
Objective—search
Objective—statistical analyses
Objective—statistics
Objective—structure
Objective—successive approximation
Objective—summarize
Objective—supportive results
Objective—suspicious
Objective—synthesis
Objective—systematic
Objective—test
Objective—theory
Objective—thesis
Objective—train
Objective—truth
Objective—unambiguous
Objective—unbiased
Objective—unchanging
Objective—uncover
Objective—understanding
Objective—unemotional
Objective—unprejudiced

Objective—utilitarian
Objective—validity
Objective—validity test
Objective—variables
Objective—verify
Objective—vigilant
Objective—wakeful
Objective—way of least resistance

PERCEPTION

Perception—part of the nemonik interaction that manages the incoming information flow from the sensory reality towards the mind. Path > nemonik thinking / interaction / **perception**

perception—Accept
perception—alert
perception—attention
perception—auditory sense
perception—detect
perception—discern
perception—early warning
perception—equilibrium sense
perception—examine
perception—explore
perception—feel
perception—five senses
perception—gustatory sense
perception—hallucination
perception—hear
perception—influence
perception—information
perception—inquire
perception—inspect
perception—interaction
perception—interest
perception—investigate
perception—kinetic sense
perception—learn
perception—listen
perception—mole
perception—nemonik thinking
perception—non-assertive
perception—non-critical
perception—non-judgmental

perception—non-verbal
perception—noticeable
perception—observe
perception—olfactory sense
perception—paraphrasing
perception—perceive
perception—perceptible
perception—probe
perception—read
perception—reconnaissance
perception—Reject
perception—scout
perception—scrutinize
perception—search
perception—see
perception—senses
perception—sensitive
perception—sensory observation
perception—sensory processes
perception—silence
perception—smell
perception—snitch
perception—solution oriented
perception—spy
perception—squealer
perception—summarize
perception—surveillance
perception—tactile sense
perception—taste
perception—thermal sense
perception—touch
perception—vigilant
perception—visual sense
perception—watch

PREPARE

Prepare—temporal nemonik that prompts the mind to get
ready for action. Path > nemonik thinking / reality / time
/ **prepare**

Prepare—allocate
Prepare—analyses
Prepare—appraise
Prepare—arrange
Prepare—calculating
Prepare—chain of command
Prepare—consequence
Prepare—coordinate
Prepare—decide
Prepare—delegate
Prepare—diagnose
Prepare—direction
Prepare—drill
Prepare—encourage
Prepare—endeavour
Prepare—enquiry
Prepare—enterprise
Prepare—equip
Prepare—estimate
Prepare—evaluate
Prepare—exercise
Prepare—finance
Prepare—follow-up
Prepare—forecast
Prepare—goal setting
Prepare—hierarchy
Prepare—inspire
Prepare—instigate
Prepare—investigate
Prepare—judgement
Prepare—know-how

Prepare—knowledge
Prepare—language
Prepare—leadership
Prepare—learn
Prepare—management
Prepare—manoeuvre
Prepare—marketing
Prepare—mission
Prepare—motivate
Prepare—nemonik thinking
Prepare—network
Prepare—operation
Prepare—organize
Prepare—planning
Prepare—positioning
Prepare—practice
Prepare—practise
Prepare—predict
Prepare—prepare
Prepare—prerequisites
Prepare—prioritizing
Prepare—prognosis
Prepare—promote
Prepare—punish
Prepare—purpose
Prepare—reality
Prepare—reorganize
Prepare—requirements
Prepare—responsible
Prepare—review
Prepare—revise
Prepare—risk avoidance
Prepare—risk management
Prepare—risk taking
Prepare—scenario
Prepare—scheduling
Prepare—schematic

Prepare—scrutinize
Prepare—search
Prepare—set goals
Prepare—skill
Prepare—stimulate
Prepare—strategy
Prepare—structure
Prepare—study
Prepare—subdivide
Prepare—subordinates
Prepare—summarize
Prepare—supervise
Prepare—supplies
Prepare—SWOT
Prepare—synchronize
Prepare—synthesize
Prepare—tactics
Prepare—target
Prepare—task setting
Prepare—time
Prepare—training
Prepare—transfer
Prepare—undertaking
Prepare—venture
Prepare—vision

PRESERVE

Preserve—material nemonik that prompts the mind to maintain the same amount of matter that is under control. Path > nemonik thinking / reality / matter / **preserve**

Preserve—animals
Preserve—assets
Preserve—atrophy
Preserve—backup
Preserve—bolthole
Preserve—capital
Preserve—care
Preserve—caretaker
Preserve—cash
Preserve—chattels
Preserve—conserve
Preserve—consolidate
Preserve—contingency
Preserve—curator
Preserve—custodian
Preserve—data
Preserve—depot
Preserve—energy
Preserve—equipment
Preserve—erosion
Preserve—facts
Preserve—figures
Preserve—fix
Preserve—fluid
Preserve—force
Preserve—fortune
Preserve—friends
Preserve—frugal
Preserve—funds
Preserve—gas
Preserve—goods

Preserve—groundskeeper
Preserve—guardian
Preserve—heal
Preserve—hideaway
Preserve—hideout
Preserve—hold
Preserve—information
Preserve—judicious
Preserve—keep up
Preserve—keeper
Preserve—knowledge
Preserve—look after
Preserve—machinery
Preserve—maintain
Preserve—material
Preserve—matter
Preserve—mend
Preserve—minder
Preserve—minding
Preserve—minerals
Preserve—money
Preserve—nemonik thinking
Preserve—numbers
Preserve—overhaul
Preserve—parsimonious
Preserve—pennywise
Preserve—people
Preserve—plants
Preserve—positioning
Preserve—preserve
Preserve—property
Preserve—protect
Preserve—prudent
Preserve—raw material
Preserve—reality
Preserve—reclaim
Preserve—recoup

Preserve—recover
Preserve—recuperate
Preserve—refurbish
Preserve—regain
Preserve—regenerate
Preserve—renew
Preserve—renovate
Preserve—repair
Preserve—replenish
Preserve—repossess
Preserve—rescue
Preserve—resources
Preserve—restore
Preserve—retain
Preserve—retention
Preserve—retrieve
Preserve—revamp
Preserve—revenue
Preserve—revitalize
Preserve—robots
Preserve—safeguard
Preserve—salvage
Preserve—sanctuary
Preserve—save
Preserve—secure
Preserve—sensible
Preserve—shelter
Preserve—spare
Preserve—staff
Preserve—standby
Preserve—statistics
Preserve—steward
Preserve—stock
Preserve—stockpile
Preserve—stockroom
Preserve—storage
Preserve—store

Preserve—storehouse
Preserve—storeroom
Preserve—supplies
Preserve—support
Preserve—sustain
Preserve—tend
Preserve—thrifty
Preserve—tools
Preserve—treasure
Preserve—upkeep
Preserve—utensils
Preserve—vehicles
Preserve—warden
Preserve—warehouse
Preserve—watchman
Preserve—wealth
Preserve—wise
Preserve—workforce

PROJECTION

Projection—part of interaction that refers to managing the outgoing information flow from the mind towards the sensory reality. Path > nemonik thinking / interaction / **projection**

projection—accuse
projection—aggressive
projection—antagonize
projection—appearance
projection—blame
projection—bluff
projection—bully
projection—callousness
projection—character
projection—charisma
projection—claim
projection—coerce
projection—Conceal
projection—confidence
projection—convince
projection—cynical
projection—declare
projection—demeanour
projection—demonstrate
projection—encourage
projection—esteem
projection—explain
projection—express
projection—eye contact
projection—facial expression
projection—firm
projection—gesticulation
projection—gestures
projection—illustrate
projection—image

projection—implore
projection—influence
projection—information
projection—insist
projection—inspire
projection—interaction
projection—intimidate
projection—lecture
projection—mana
projection—mannerisms
projection—motivate
projection—nemonik thinking
projection—non-verbal
projection—persistent
projection—persuade
projection—plead
projection—pledge
projection—polite
projection—posture
projection—present
projection—prestige
projection—proclaim
projection—prominence
projection—promise
projection—promote
projection—pronounce
projection—prove
projection—provoke
projection—publish
projection—reassure
projection—recognition
projection—relax
projection—reputation
projection—respect
projection—Reveal
projection—sarcastic
projection—scare

projection—show
projection—speak
projection—stance
projection—status
projection—stimulate
projection—submissive
projection—support
projection—sway
projection—swear
projection—tact
projection—talk
projection—terror
projection—threat
projection—torment
projection—transmit
projection—trap
projection—unambiguous
projection—unemotional
projection—write

RATIONAL THINKING

Rational thinking—conscious part of nemonik thinking that deals with the predictable order of reality by submitting facts to reason in order to create new facts. Path > nemonik thinking / mind / conscious / **rational thinking**

rational thinking—analyses
rational thinking—antitheses
rational thinking—Aristotle
rational thinking—artificial intelligence
rational thinking—attention
rational thinking—calculating
rational thinking—categories
rational thinking—causation
rational thinking—cause
rational thinking—cause-effect
rational thinking—certain
rational thinking—cognitive
rational thinking—coherent
rational thinking—Collective
rational thinking—comprehension
rational thinking—computable
rational thinking—concentrate
rational thinking—conclusion
rational thinking—conscious
rational thinking—consequence
rational thinking—consistent
rational thinking—contemplating
rational thinking—convincing
rational thinking—correct
rational thinking—countable
rational thinking—critical
rational thinking—cynical
rational thinking—data
rational thinking—deductive
rational thinking—details

rational thinking—deterministic
rational thinking—diagnose
rational thinking—dialectic
rational thinking—disbelieve
rational thinking—dispassion
rational thinking—distrust
rational thinking—doubt
rational thinking—efficient
rational thinking—effortless
rational thinking—emotionless
rational thinking—enquiry
rational thinking—eternal truth
rational thinking—evaluate
rational thinking—evidence
rational thinking—exact
rational thinking—examine
rational thinking—extend
rational thinking—extrapolate
rational thinking—facts
rational thinking—factual
rational thinking—figures
rational thinking—focus
rational thinking—formal logic
rational thinking—Hegel, F.
rational thinking—if-then arguments
rational thinking—impartial
rational thinking—impersonal
rational thinking—inductive
rational thinking—inference
rational thinking—inquiry
rational thinking—interpolate
rational thinking—investigate
rational thinking—judgement
rational thinking—knowledge
rational thinking—law of causality
rational thinking—laws
rational thinking—least effort

rational thinking—least resistance
rational thinking—level-headed
rational thinking—logic
rational thinking—maximize
rational thinking—measureable
rational thinking—methodical
rational thinking—mind
rational thinking—minimum effort
rational thinking—mistrust
rational thinking—nemonik accelerator
rational thinking—nemonik thinking
rational thinking—neutral
rational thinking—numbers
rational thinking—Objective
rational thinking—Ockham's razor
rational thinking—order
rational thinking—organize
rational thinking—pattern
rational thinking—practical
rational thinking—precise
rational thinking—predict
rational thinking—premise
rational thinking—probability
rational thinking—probe
rational thinking—professional
rational thinking—quantifiable
rational thinking—question
rational thinking—reason
rational thinking—reliable
rational thinking—results
rational thinking—review
rational thinking—sceptic
rational thinking—schematic
rational thinking—scrutinize
rational thinking—sequential
rational thinking—software
rational thinking—statistics

rational thinking—structure
rational thinking—successive approximation
rational thinking—suspicious
rational thinking—synthesis
rational thinking—systematic
rational thinking—thesis
rational thinking—truth
rational thinking—unbiased
rational thinking—uncover
rational thinking—understanding
rational thinking—unemotional
rational thinking—utilitarian
rational thinking—valid
rational thinking—variables
rational thinking—verify
rational thinking—vigilant
rational thinking—way of least resistance

REACTIVE

Reactive—(1) mental nemonik referring to the reactive mindmode. (2) Mental or physical response without conscious thinking that is initiated by the reactive mindmode. See Reactive mindmode. Path > nemonik thinking / mind / subconscious / affectorial thinking / **reactive**

Reactive—ability
Reactive—accurate
Reactive—accuse
Reactive—accustom
Reactive—adept
Reactive—affecters
Reactive—affectorial thinking
Reactive—aggressive
Reactive—algorithm
Reactive—alpha brainwaves
Reactive—alpha-state
Reactive—anticipate
Reactive—aphorisms
Reactive—argument
Reactive—arrogance
Reactive—attitude
Reactive—automatic process
Reactive—axioms
Reactive—behaviour
Reactive—being
Reactive—belief
Reactive—believe
Reactive—biofeedback
Reactive—blame
Reactive—bluff
Reactive—body posture
Reactive—brainwashed
Reactive—break
Reactive—breather

Reactive—bright
Reactive—brilliant
Reactive—bully
Reactive—calm
Reactive—catnap
Reactive—certain
Reactive—character
Reactive—charisma
Reactive—closed mind
Reactive—cognitive
Reactive—cognitive dissonance
Reactive—common sense
Reactive—competence
Reactive—compulsion
Reactive—condition
Reactive—confidence
Reactive—consistent
Reactive—constant
Reactive—control
Reactive—coordinate
Reactive—correct
Reactive—craving
Reactive—decision
Reactive—delusion
Reactive—demeanour
Reactive—determination
Reactive—deterministic
Reactive—devotion
Reactive—dexterity
Reactive—dogmatic
Reactive—doze
Reactive—drill
Reactive—drive
Reactive—efficient
Reactive—effortless
Reactive—ego
Reactive—egoism

Reactive—emergency
Reactive—emotion
Reactive—empty mind
Reactive—exercise
Reactive—expectation
Reactive—experience
Reactive—expert
Reactive—eye contact
Reactive—facial expression
Reactive—faith
Reactive—familiar
Reactive—fast
Reactive—feelings
Reactive—flawless
Reactive—folk's wisdom
Reactive—genius
Reactive—gifted
Reactive—gut feeling
Reactive—habituation
Reactive—hallucination
Reactive—heuristics
Reactive—hidden
Reactive—hunch
Reactive—hypnosis
Reactive—I
Reactive—identity
Reactive—illogical
Reactive—illusion
Reactive—impatient
Reactive—impulse
Reactive—inaccessible
Reactive—inactive
Reactive—inclination
Reactive—individual
Reactive—inflexible
Reactive—informal logic
Reactive—inner self

Reactive—insight
Reactive—instinct
Reactive—internalization
Reactive—internalize
Reactive—intuition
Reactive—intuitive thinking
Reactive—involuntarily
Reactive—irrational
Reactive—katas
Reactive—knowledge
Reactive—Lao Zi
Reactive—learn
Reactive—least effort
Reactive—least resistance
Reactive—mana
Reactive—mannerisms
Reactive—maturation
Reactive—maximize
Reactive—maxims
Reactive—me
Reactive—meditation
Reactive—memory
Reactive—mental habituation
Reactive—mental model
Reactive—mental perfection
Reactive—mental process
Reactive—mental reorganization
Reactive—methodical
Reactive—mind
Reactive—mind management
Reactive—mind control
Reactive—mindpower
Reactive—mindset
Reactive—mindware
Reactive—minimum effort
Reactive—mistrust
Reactive—mnemonic

Reactive—motivate
Reactive—myself
Reactive—napping
Reactive—nemonik thinking
Reactive—neural plasticity
Reactive—non-critical
Reactive—non-judgmental
Reactive—oblivious
Reactive—open mind
Reactive—optimization
Reactive—order
Reactive—organize
Reactive—overload protection
Reactive—peaceful
Reactive—perfection
Reactive—persistent
Reactive—persona
Reactive—personal
Reactive—personality
Reactive—physical habituation
Reactive—physical perfection
Reactive—polite
Reactive—posture
Reactive—practice
Reactive—practise
Reactive—pragmatic
Reactive—precise
Reactive—predict
Reactive—predictable
Reactive—predisposition
Reactive—premonition
Reactive—presentiment
Reactive—proficiency
Reactive—programmed
Reactive—progress
Reactive—prompt
Reactive—quick

Reactive—rapid
Reactive—rash
Reactive—reaction
Reactive—Reactive
Reactive—reactive
Reactive—reactive affecter
Reactive—reactive mindmode
Reactive—reflex
Reactive—regret
Reactive—relax
Reactive—reliable
Reactive—remember
Reactive—remorse
Reactive—repetition
Reactive—repetitive behaviours
Reactive—repetitive thoughts
Reactive—resolution
Reactive—resolve
Reactive—responsive
Reactive—rest
Reactive—rigid
Reactive—roused
Reactive—routine
Reactive—rule of thumb
Reactive—self
Reactive—self-confidence
Reactive—self-conscious
Reactive—self-control
Reactive—self-discipline
Reactive—self-doubt
Reactive—self-hypnosis
Reactive—selfish
Reactive—selfless
Reactive—semiconscious
Reactive—semiconscious dominance
Reactive—sensations
Reactive—sensible

Reactive—serenity
Reactive—set of rules
Reactive—silent mind
Reactive—single-minded
Reactive—sixth sense
Reactive—skill
Reactive—sleep
Reactive—slumber
Reactive—soul
Reactive—specialist
Reactive—speed
Reactive—spirit
Reactive—stable
Reactive—stagnant
Reactive—static
Reactive—status quo
Reactive—stubborn
Reactive—study
Reactive—subconscious
Reactive—subjective
Reactive—successive approximation
Reactive—suggestibility
Reactive—sway
Reactive—swift
Reactive—systematic
Reactive—talent
Reactive—time-out
Reactive—train
Reactive—training
Reactive—traits
Reactive—tranquillity
Reactive—trust
Reactive—truth
Reactive—twilight state
Reactive—unaware
Reactive—unchanging
Reactive—uncritical

Reactive—unknown
Reactive—unreasonable
Reactive—unsubstantiated
Reactive—unsystematic
Reactive—unwind
Reactive—unyielding
Reactive—vigilant
Reactive—virtuoso
Reactive—volition
Reactive—way of least resistance
Reactive—will
Reactive—willpower
Reactive—wisdom
Reactive—wizard
Reactive—wunderkind
Reactive—zone

REALITY

Reality—See External reality.

REJECT

Reject—perceptual nemonik that prompts the mind to refuse the incoming information as a true description of the sensory reality. Path > nemonik thinking / interaction / perception / **reject**

Reject—abandon
Reject—accuse
Reject—aggressive
Reject—antagonize
Reject—antitheses
Reject—averse
Reject—ban
Reject—bar
Reject—blame
Reject—bully
Reject—calculating
Reject—callousness
Reject—cancel
Reject—careful
Reject—cautious
Reject—censor
Reject—choice
Reject—closed mind
Reject—communicate
Reject—condemn
Reject—conflict
Reject—contempt
Reject—contradict
Reject—conversation
Reject—criticize
Reject—data
Reject—decline
Reject—decry
Reject—defame
Reject—degrade

Reject—denigrate
Reject—denounce
Reject—deny
Reject—details
Reject—diagnose
Reject—different
Reject—disaccord
Reject—disagreement
Reject—disallow
Reject—disapprove
Reject—disbelieve
Reject—discard
Reject—discontent
Reject—discord
Reject—discount
Reject—disgruntled
Reject—disinclined
Reject—dislike
Reject—dismiss
Reject—disparage
Reject—displeased
Reject—disprove
Reject—dispute
Reject—disregard
Reject—dissent
Reject—distaste
Reject—distrust
Reject—doubt
Reject—dubious
Reject—except
Reject—exclude
Reject—facts
Reject—figures
Reject—forbid
Reject—hinder
Reject—ignore
Reject—inflexible

Reject—inhibit
Reject—injunction
Reject—interaction
Reject—interdict
Reject—intransigent
Reject—loathing
Reject—mistrust
Reject—narrow-minded
Reject—nemonik thinking
Reject—numbers
Reject—objection
Reject—obstinate
Reject—omit
Reject—opposition
Reject—ostracise
Reject—outcast
Reject—outlaw
Reject—overrule
Reject—paranoid
Reject—Perception
Reject—pig-headed
Reject—prevent
Reject—prohibit
Reject—proscribe
Reject—provoke
Reject—quarrelsome
Reject—rebel
Reject—rebut
Reject—refuse
Reject—reject
Reject—risk avoidance
Reject—sanction
Reject—sceptic
Reject—scorn
Reject—selfish
Reject—stagnant
Reject—static

Reject—strict
Reject—suspicious
Reject—threat
Reject—unconvinced
Reject—unimpressed
Reject—uninterested
Reject—unmoved
Reject—unresolved
Reject—unsympathetic
Reject—unwillingness
Reject—unyielding
Reject—veto
Reject—wary

RETREAT

Retreat—spatial nemonik that prompts the mind to increase the distance to the goal. Path > nemonik thinking / reality / space / **retreat**

Retreat—abandon
Retreat—abscond
Retreat—apologize
Retreat—attenuate
Retreat—backslide
Retreat—backward
Retreat—capitulate
Retreat—cessation
Retreat—collapse
Retreat—compromise
Retreat—concede
Retreat—constriction
Retreat—contract
Retreat—crumble
Retreat—decline
Retreat—decrease
Retreat—defeat
Retreat—defect
Retreat—demise
Retreat—demote
Retreat—depart
Retreat—descend
Retreat—desert
Retreat—diminish
Retreat—disappear
Retreat—disconnect
Retreat—disengage
Retreat—disintegrate
Retreat—dissociate
Retreat—dissolution
Retreat—divorce

Retreat—downfall
Retreat—downgrade
Retreat—dwindle
Retreat—escape
Retreat—evacuate
Retreat—evade
Retreat—exit
Retreat—exodus
Retreat—fade
Retreat—fail
Retreat—fall-back
Retreat—flee
Retreat—forfeiture
Retreat—forsake
Retreat—give up
Retreat—known territory
Retreat—leave
Retreat—lose
Retreat—momentum
Retreat—nemonik thinking
Retreat—non-assertive
Retreat—outflanked
Retreat—outrun
Retreat—overrun
Retreat—parting
Retreat—positioning
Retreat—pullback
Retreat—reality
Retreat—rear-guard
Retreat—recall
Retreat—recede
Retreat—recoil
Retreat—recover
Retreat—recuperate
Retreat—reduce
Retreat—regress
Retreat—regroup

Retreat—relinquish
Retreat—relocate
Retreat—reorganize
Retreat—reposition
Retreat—resign
Retreat—restrict
Retreat—restructure
Retreat—retire
Retreat—retract
Retreat—retreat
Retreat—return
Retreat—reverse
Retreat—rout
Retreat—setback
Retreat—shorten supply-lines
Retreat—shrink
Retreat—shrivel
Retreat—space
Retreat—speed
Retreat—subside
Retreat—supply lines
Retreat—surrender
Retreat—survival
Retreat—turnaround
Retreat—vacate
Retreat—vanish
Retreat—wane
Retreat—withdraw,
Retreat—wither

REVEAL

Reveal—projectional nemonik that prompts the mind to project true information to the sensory reality. Path > nemonik thinking / interaction / projection / **reveal**

Reveal—accuse
Reveal—advertise
Reveal—announce
Reveal—antagonize
Reveal—appearance
Reveal—argument
Reveal—assertive
Reveal—assure
Reveal—audience
Reveal—authoritive
Reveal—blame
Reveal—bluff
Reveal—body posture
Reveal—books
Reveal—broadcast
Reveal—bully
Reveal—candid
Reveal—careless
Reveal—character
Reveal—charisma
Reveal—choice
Reveal—claim
Reveal—clarify
Reveal—clear
Reveal—coach
Reveal—coerce
Reveal—communicate
Reveal—confidence
Reveal—conversation
Reveal—convince
Reveal—counsel

Reveal—critical
Reveal—cynical
Reveal—data
Reveal—declare
Reveal—deliberate
Reveal—demeanour
Reveal—demonstrate
Reveal—dependable
Reveal—details
Reveal—disclose
Reveal—display
Reveal—divulge
Reveal—educate
Reveal—encourage
Reveal—enlighten
Reveal—esteem
Reveal—exhibit
Reveal—explain
Reveal—expose
Reveal—express
Reveal—eye contact
Reveal—facial expression
Reveal—facts
Reveal—figures
Reveal—frank
Reveal—gesticulation
Reveal—gestures
Reveal—honest
Reveal—honourable
Reveal—illustrate
Reveal—image
Reveal—implore
Reveal—influence
Reveal—inform
Reveal—information
Reveal—insist
Reveal—inspire

Reveal—instruct
Reveal—interaction
Reveal—intimidate
Reveal—knowledge
Reveal—language
Reveal—leak
Reveal—lecture
Reveal—letters
Reveal—loyal
Reveal—mana
Reveal—mannerisms
Reveal—messages
Reveal—motivate
Reveal—nemonik thinking
Reveal—numbers
Reveal—open
Reveal—pacify
Reveal—persistent
Reveal—persuade
Reveal—plead
Reveal—pledge
Reveal—polite
Reveal—posture
Reveal—present
Reveal—prestige
Reveal—proclaim
Reveal—projection
Reveal—promise
Reveal—promote
Reveal—pronounce
Reveal—prove
Reveal—provoke
Reveal—publicity
Reveal—publish
Reveal—Reactive
Reveal—reassure
Reveal—release

Reveal—reliable
Reveal—reputation
Reveal—respect
Reveal—responsible
Reveal—reveal
Reveal—sarcastic
Reveal—scare
Reveal—sensitive
Reveal—show
Reveal—speak
Reveal—stance
Reveal—status
Reveal—stimulate
Reveal—straightforward
Reveal—support
Reveal—sway
Reveal—swear
Reveal—tact
Reveal—talk
Reveal—teach
Reveal—tell
Reveal—terror
Reveal—torment
Reveal—trust
Reveal—trustworthy
Reveal—tutor
Reveal—unveil
Reveal—upfront
Reveal—warn
Reveal—whistle-blower,
Reveal—win-win
Reveal—write

SEMICONSCIOUS

Semiconscious—part of the mind that comprises parts of the conscious and subconscious, which form a communication channel between those parts of the mind. Path > nemonik thinking / mind / **semiconscious**

semiconscious—activate subconscious
semiconscious—alpha brainwaves
semiconscious—alpha-state
semiconscious—biofeedback
semiconscious—bypass conscious
semiconscious—calm
semiconscious—catnap
semiconscious—confidence
semiconscious—Creative
semiconscious—doze
semiconscious—empty mind
semiconscious—hypnosis
semiconscious—inhibit conscious
semiconscious—internalize
semiconscious—meditation
semiconscious—memory
semiconscious—mental state
semiconscious—mind
semiconscious—mind management
semiconscious—napping
semiconscious—nemonik thinking
semiconscious—peaceful
semiconscious—Reactive
semiconscious—relax
semiconscious—rest
semiconscious—self-hypnosis
semiconscious—semiconscious dominance
semiconscious—serenity
semiconscious—silent mind
semiconscious—sleep

semiconscious—slumber
semiconscious—subconscious
semiconscious—suggestibility
semiconscious—tranquil
semiconscious—twilight state
semiconscious—unwind
semiconscious—zone

SENSORY REALITY

Sensory reality—part of the external reality that can be perceived directly through the natural human senses. Path > nemonik thinking / **reality**

sensory reality—Accumulate
sensory reality—Act
sensory reality—Advance
sensory reality—auditory
sensory reality—concrete
sensory reality—detectable
sensory reality—Dispose
sensory reality—exterior
sensory reality—external
sensory reality—gustatory
sensory reality—hear
sensory reality—impartial
sensory reality—interaction
sensory reality—kinetic
sensory reality—material
sensory reality—material body
sensory reality—matter
sensory reality—nemonik thinking
sensory reality—Newtonian sensory reality
sensory reality—normal
sensory reality—olfactory
sensory reality—Prepare
sensory reality—Preserve
sensory reality—real
sensory reality—realism
sensory reality—realistic
sensory reality—reasonable
sensory reality—Retreat
sensory reality—see
sensory reality—senses
sensory reality—smell

sensory reality—space
sensory reality—spatial
sensory reality—Stay
sensory reality—tactile
sensory reality—taste
sensory reality—temporal
sensory reality—thermal
sensory reality—time
sensory reality—touch
sensory reality—visual
sensory reality—Wait

SPACE

Space—three-dimensional, infinite, and nonmaterial part of
reality in which matter is immersed and moves around.
Path > nemonik thinking / reality / **space**

space—Advance
space—altitude
space—area
space—boundary
space—coordinates
space—cosmos
space—distance
space—elevation
space—here
space—infinite
space—latitude
space—limitless
space—location
space—longitude
space—mobile
space—momentum
space—motion
space—movement
space—nemonik thinking
space—nonmaterial
space—outflank
space—outmanoeuvre
space—outrun
space—overrun
space—overthrow
space—overwhelm
space—permanent
space—perpetual
space—place
space—point
space—position

space—reality
space—Retreat
space—site
space—spatial management
space—speed
space—Stay
space—there
space—three-dimensional
space—trajectory
space—transfer
space—transport
space—travel
space—universe
space—unsubstantial
space—Wait
space—where

STAY

Stay—spatial nemonik that prompts the mind to maintain the same distance to the goal. Path > nemonik thinking / reality / space / **stay**

Stay—breakdown
Stay—captured
Stay—caught
Stay—cessation
Stay—comfort zone
Stay—confined
Stay—consolidate
Stay—custody
Stay—defend
Stay—delay
Stay—detain
Stay—embed
Stay—entrench
Stay—fixed
Stay—fortify
Stay—frozen
Stay—halt
Stay—idle
Stay—immobile
Stay—inactive
Stay—incarcerated
Stay—inert
Stay—inflexible
Stay—ingrained
Stay—inoperative
Stay—lethargic
Stay—lifeless
Stay—malfunction
Stay—motionless
Stay—nemonik thinking
Stay—out of action

Stay—out of order
Stay—paralysed
Stay—passive
Stay—pause
Stay—positioning
Stay—postpone
Stay—procrastinate
Stay—protect
Stay—reality
Stay—recover
Stay—recuperate
Stay—relax
Stay—repose
Stay—rest
Stay—rigid
Stay—sentinel
Stay—sentry
Stay—set
Stay—shelter
Stay—space
Stay—stagnant
Stay—stall
Stay—standby
Stay—standstill
Stay—static
Stay—stationary
Stay—stay
Stay—supply lines
Stay—time-out
Stay—unchanging
Stay—unmoving
Stay—unused
Stay—unyielding

SUBCONSCIOUS

Subconscious—large part of the mind that is continuously active outside the conscious awareness of that person. Path > nemonik thinking / mind / **subconscious**

subconscious—affectorial thinking
subconscious—alpha brainwaves
subconscious—alpha-state
subconscious—break
subconscious—breather
subconscious—bright
subconscious—brilliant
subconscious—calm
subconscious—catnap
subconscious—character
subconscious—charisma
subconscious—confidence
subconscious—Creative
subconscious—defragmentation
subconscious—doze
subconscious—empty mind
subconscious—exercise
subconscious—genius
subconscious—gifted
subconscious—hidden
subconscious—hypnosis
subconscious—idle
subconscious—inaccessible
subconscious—inactive
subconscious—individual
subconscious—inert
subconscious—inoperative
subconscious—intelligent
subconscious—internalize
subconscious—learn
subconscious—meditation

subconscious—memory
subconscious—mental reorganization
subconscious—mental signals
subconscious—mental state
subconscious—mind
subconscious—mind management
subconscious—mindpower
subconscious—mnemonic
subconscious—mystery
subconscious—napping
subconscious—nemonik thinking
subconscious—neural plasticity
subconscious—oblivious
subconscious—obscured
subconscious—organize
subconscious—overload protection
subconscious—peaceful
subconscious—Reactive
subconscious—relax
subconscious—repose
subconscious—rest
subconscious—sealed
subconscious—self
subconscious—self-hypnosis
subconscious—semiconscious
subconscious—semiconscious dominance
subconscious—silent mind
subconscious—sleep
subconscious—slumber
subconscious—suggestibility
subconscious—talent
subconscious—time-out
subconscious—train
subconscious—tranquillity
subconscious—twilight state
subconscious—unaware
subconscious—unknown

subconscious—unwind
subconscious—virtuoso
subconscious—wizard
subconscious—wunderkind
subconscious—zone

SUCCESS

Success—obtain what you seek and escape what you suffer (Lao Zi). Success is goal oriented and, therefore, it fosters compassion, allies, and win-win strategies. Antonym— Winning.

success—accomplishment
success—achievement
success—allies
success—associates
success—attainment
success—buddies
success—compassion
success—cronies
success—escape
success—feat
success—followers
success—friends
success—fulfilment
success—goal oriented
success—happiness
success—helpers
success—Lao Zi
success—mission
success—need
success—obtain
success—partners
success—realization
success—seek
success—supporters
success—survival
success—win-win strategies

THINKING

Thinking is a self-organizing mental process that recalls, evaluates, transforms, and generates information.

thinking—associate
thinking—brain
thinking—brainware
thinking—cognitive
thinking—conscious
thinking—defragmentation
thinking—mental process
thinking—mind
thinking—neural plasticity
thinking—problem solving
thinking—prompt thinking
thinking—self-organizing
thinking—strategical thinking
thinking—structural thinking
thinking—systematic thinking
thinking—tactical thinking
thinking—train

TIME

Time—one-dimensional, eternal, and nonmaterial part of reality that can be perceived indirectly by changes in matter and the movement of matter through space. Path > nemonik thinking / reality / **time**

time—Act
time—after
time—ancient
time—before
time—chronological
time—contemporary
time—current
time—duration
time—earlier
time—eternal
time—everlasting
time—flowing
time—forever
time—former
time—future
time—history
time—immediately
time—imminent
time—impending
time—instantly
time—interminable
time—interval
time—later
time—linear
time—modern
time—moment
time—nemonik thinking
time—never-ending
time—next
time—nonmaterial

time—now
time—old
time—one-dimensional
time—past
time—period
time—permanent
time—perpetual
time—preceding
time—Prepare
time—present
time—previous
time—prior
time—progressing
time—reality
time—sequential
time—temporal
time—time management
time—timeless
time—timely
time—time-out
time—timing
time—today
time—tomorrow
time—unending
time—unsubstantial
time—upcoming
time—urgent
time—Wait
time—when
time—yesterday

WAIT

Wait—temporal nemonik that prompts the mind to delay an action until it is the right time for that action. Path > nemonik thinking / reality / time / **wait**

Wait—adjourn
Wait—armistice
Wait—break
Wait—careful
Wait—cautious
Wait—ceasefire
Wait—cessation
Wait—cowardice
Wait—delay
Wait—hesitant
Wait—idle
Wait—inactive
Wait—indecisive
Wait—inert
Wait—inoperative
Wait—insecure
Wait—interim
Wait—interlude
Wait—intermezzo
Wait—intermission
Wait—interrupt
Wait—interval
Wait—irresolute
Wait—lazy
Wait—lethargic
Wait—lull
Wait—nemonik thinking
Wait—non-assertive
Wait—paralysis
Wait—patience
Wait—pause

Wait—pending
Wait—positioning
Wait—postpone
Wait—procrastinate
Wait—prolong
Wait—put on hold
Wait—reality
Wait—recess
Wait—relax
Wait—reluctant
Wait—repose
Wait—reprieve
Wait—rest
Wait—restrain
Wait—right moment
Wait—risk avoidance
Wait—safety
Wait—secure
Wait—slack
Wait—stagnant
Wait—stall
Wait—stationary
Wait—suspend
Wait—time
Wait—time off
Wait—uncommitted
Wait—unconfident
Wait—unfamiliar
Wait—unproductive
Wait—unsure
Wait—vacation
Wait—wait
Wait—wary
Wait—wavering

WINNING

Winning—defeating opponents in competition and, therefore, winning is conflict oriented, which fosters control,
force, aggression, enemies, and win-lose strategies. Antonym—Success.

winning—adversaries
winning—aggression
winning—antagonists
winning—argument
winning—battle
winning—beating
winning—bout
winning—clash
winning—combat
winning—competition
winning—conflict oriented
winning—confrontation
winning—conquest
winning—contest
winning—coup
winning—debate
winning—defeating
winning—disagreement
winning—dispute
winning—enemies
winning—fight
winning—foes
winning—glee
winning—gloat
winning—landslide
winning—match
winning—nemeses
winning—opponents
winning—overthrow
winning—quarrel

winning—rivals
winning—round
winning—rout
winning—row
winning—squabble
winning—subjugation
winning—takeover
winning—triumph
winning—victory
winning—war
winning—warfare
winning—win-lose strategies

Notes

PART-II: KEYWORDS TO NEMONIKS

A – KEYWORDS

abandon—Dispose
abandon—Reject
abandon—Retreat
abide—Accept
ability—Reactive
abscond—Retreat
abundance—Accumulate
accede—Accept
accept—Accept
accept—interaction
accept—nemonik
accept—nemonik thinking
accept—perception
accomplish—nemonik thinking
accomplishment—success
accord—Accept
accrue—Accumulate
accumulate—Accumulate
accumulate—matter
accumulate—nemonik
accumulate—nemonik thinking
accumulate—reality
accurate—Collective
accurate—Objective
accurate—Reactive
accuse—Collective
accuse—projection
accuse—Reactive
accuse—Reject
accuse—Reveal
accustom—Accept
accustom—Reactive
achieve—nemonik thinking
achievement—success
acquiesce—Accept

acquire—Accumulate
act—Act
act—nemonik
act—nemonik thinking
act—reality
act—time
add—Accumulate
adept—Reactive
adjourn—Wait
adjust—Accept
adjust—Collective
administration—Collective
admit—Accept
adore—Accept
advance—Advance
advance—Creative
advance—nemonik
advance—nemonik thinking
advance—reality
advance—space
adversaries—winning
advertise—Reveal
advocate—Accept
affecters—beliefs
affecters—Creative
affecters—desires
affecters—discoveries
affecters—emotions
affecters—fantasies
affecters—habits
affecters—heuristics
affecters—ideas
affecters—impulses
affecters—innovations
affecters—insights,
affecters—inspirations
affecters—intuitions

affecters—inventions
affecters—mental signals
affecters—novelties
affecters—reactions
affecters—Reactive
affecters—reflexes
affecters—routines
affecters—skills
affection—Accept
affectorial thinking—nemonik thinking
affluence—Accumulate
after—time
aggression—Collective
aggression—conventional thinking
aggression—winning
aggressive—Accumulate
aggressive—Act
aggressive—Advance
aggressive—Conceal
aggressive—projection
aggressive—Reactive
aggressive—Reject
agreement—Accept
agreement—Collective
aid—Collective
alert—Collective
alert—Objective
alert—perception
algorithm—Reactive
align—Accept
alliance—Collective
allies—success
all-inclusive—nemonik thinking
allocate—Prepare
allow—Accept
alpha brainwaves—affectorial thinking
alpha brainwaves—Creative

alpha brainwaves—Reactive
alpha brainwaves—semiconscious
alpha brainwaves—subconscious
alpha-state—affectorial thinking
alpha-state—Creative
alpha-state—Reactive
alpha-state—semiconscious
alpha-state—subconscious
alterable—Collective
alternatives—Creative
altitude—space
amalgamate—Collective
amass—Accumulate
ambiguity—interaction
ambush—Conceal
amendable—Collective
amiable—Accept
Analects—Collective
analyses—Collective
analyses—Objective
analyses—Prepare
analyses—rational thinking
ancient—time
animals—Accumulate
animals—Dispose
animals—matter
animals—Preserve
annex—Accumulate
annihilate—Dispose
announce—Reveal
answering—conventional thinking
antagonists—winning
antagonize—Accumulate
antagonize—Act
antagonize—Advance
antagonize—projection
antagonize—Reject

antagonize—Reveal
anticipate—Collective
anticipate—Creative
anticipate—mind
anticipate—Objective
anticipate—Reactive
antitheses—Collective
antitheses—Objective
antitheses—rational thinking
antitheses—Reject
aphorisms—Reactive
apologize—Retreat
appearance—Conceal
appearance—projection
appearance—Reveal
appease—Accept
appraise—Prepare
appreciate—Accept
approve—Accept
arbitrary—Collective
area—space
argument—Collective
argument—Objective
argument—Reactive
argument—Reveal
argument—winning
Aristotle—Collective
Aristotle—Objective
Aristotle—rational thinking
arithmetic—Objective
armistice—Wait
arrange—Prepare
arrangement—Collective
arrogance—Reactive
artificial—Collective
artificial intelligence—Collective
artificial intelligence—Objective

artificial intelligence—rational thinking
artistic—Creative
assassinate—Dispose
assault—Advance
assemble—Accumulate
assemble—Collective
assertive—Reveal
assets—Accumulate
assets—Dispose
assets—matter
assets—Preserve
assistance—Collective
associate—Collective
associate—memory
associate—nemonik
associate—nemonik thinking
associate—thinking
associates—success
assure—Reveal
atrophy—Preserve
attack—Advance
attain—Accumulate
attainment—success
attention—Collective
attention—conscious
attention—Objective
attention—perception
attention—rational thinking
attenuate—Retreat
attitude—Reactive
attorney—Collective
audience—Collective
audience—Reveal
auditory—reality
auditory sense—perception
augment—Accumulate
authenticate—Accept

authoritive—Reveal
authority—Collective
authorize—Accept
automatic process—nemonik thinking
automatic process—Reactive
averse—Reject
avoid—Conceal
awake—Collective
awake—conscious
awake—Objective
aware—Collective
aware—conscious
aware—Objective
axioms—Reactive

B – KEYWORDS

backslide—Retreat
backup—Preserve
backward—Retreat
bamboozle—Conceal
bamboozled—Accept
ban—Dispose
ban—Reject
bar—Reject
barrister—Collective
battle—winning
beating—winning
before—time
behaviour—Collective
behaviour—Creative
behaviour—mind
behaviour—Objective
behaviour—Reactive
being—mind
being—Reactive
belief—Reactive
beliefs—nemonik thinking
believe—Reactive
belonging—Collective
benevolent—Accept
betray—Conceal
betrayed—Accept
biofeedback—Creative
biofeedback—Reactive
biofeedback—semiconscious
blame—projection
blame—Reactive
blame—Reject
blame—Reveal
blind-sight—Conceal
bluff—Collective

bluff—projection
bluff—Reactive
bluff—Reveal
body—matter
body language—Collective
body language—interaction
body posture—Collective
body posture—interaction
body posture—Reactive
body posture—Reveal
bolthole—Preserve
books—Collective
books—interaction
books—Reveal
borrow—Accumulate
boundary—space
bout—winning
brain—memory
brain—mind
brain—nemonik
brain—nemonik thinking
brain—thinking
brainstorming—Creative
brainware—memory
brainware—mind
brainware—nemonik
brainware—nemonik thinking
brainware—thinking
brainwashed—Reactive
brainwashing—Collective
brave—Act
break—Creative
break—Reactive
break—subconscious
break—Wait
break into—Advance
breakdown—Stay

breather—Creative
breather—Reactive
breather—subconscious
breed—Accumulate
bright—Creative
bright—Reactive
bright—subconscious
brilliant—Creative
brilliant—Reactive
brilliant—subconscious
broadcast—Reveal
buddies—success
build—Accumulate
bully—Accumulate
bully—Act
bully—Advance
bully—projection
bully—Reactive
bully—Reject
bully—Reveal
bureaucracy—Collective
burn—Dispose
business—Collective
buy—Accumulate
bypass—Advance
bypass conscious—semiconscious

C – KEYWORDS

calculating—Collective
calculating—Conceal
calculating—Objective
calculating—Prepare
calculating—rational thinking
calculating—Reject
callousness—Collective
callousness—Conceal
callousness—Objective
callousness—projection
callousness—Reject
calm—affectorial thinking
calm—Creative
calm—Reactive
calm—semiconscious
calm—subconscious
camaraderie—Collective
camouflage—Conceal
cancel—Reject
candid—Reveal
capital—Accumulate
capital—Dispose
capital—matter
capital—Preserve
capitulate—Retreat
capture—Accumulate
captured—Stay
care—Collective
care—Preserve
careful—Conceal
careful—Reject
careful—Wait
careless—Accept
careless—Act
careless—Reveal

caretaker—Preserve
carry out—Act
cash—Accumulate
cash—Dispose
cash—matter
cash—Preserve
cast off—Dispose
catch—Accumulate
categories—Collective
categories—Objective
categories—rational thinking
catnap—affectorial thinking
catnap—Creative
catnap—Reactive
catnap—semiconscious
catnap—subconscious
caught—Stay
causation—Collective
causation—Objective
causation—rational thinking
cause—Collective
cause—Objective
cause—rational thinking
cause-effect—Collective
cause-effect—Objective
cause-effect—rational thinking
cautious—Reject
cautious—Wait
ceasefire—Wait
censor—Conceal
censor—Reject
certain—Collective
certain—Objective
certain—rational thinking
certain—Reactive
cessation—Retreat
cessation—Stay

cessation—Wait
chain of command—Collective
chain of command—Prepare
changeable—Collective
chaos—Creative
character—affectorial thinking
character—mind
character—projection
character—Reactive
character—Reveal
character—subconscious
charge—Advance
charisma—affectorial thinking
charisma—interaction
charisma—mind
charisma—projection
charisma—Reactive
charisma—Reveal
charisma—subconscious
chase—Advance
chattels—Accumulate
chattels—Dispose
chattels—matter
chattels—Preserve
cheat—Conceal
cheated—Accept
choice—Accept
choice—Conceal
choice—mind
choice—Reject
choice—Reveal
chronological—time
circumference—matter
civil law—Collective
civil service—Collective
claim—Accumulate
claim—Advance

claim—Collective
claim—projection
claim—Reveal
clarify—Reveal
clash—winning
clear—Dispose
clear—Reveal
climate change—conventional thinking
cloak—Conceal
closed mind—mind
closed mind—Reactive
closed mind—Reject
closeness—Collective
club—Collective
coach—Reveal
coalition—Collective
code—interaction
code of conduct—Collective
coerce—Collective
coerce—projection
coerce—Reveal
cognitive—Collective
cognitive—Creative
cognitive—mind
cognitive—nemonik
cognitive—nemonik thinking
cognitive—Objective
cognitive—rational thinking
cognitive—Reactive
cognitive—thinking
cognitive dissonance—Reactive
cognizant—conscious
coherent—Collective
coherent—Objective
coherent—rational thinking
collaborate—Collective
collapse—Retreat

collective—Collective
collective—conscious
collective—mind
collective—mindmode
collective—nemonik
collective—nemonik thinking
collective—rational thinking
collective truth—Collective
combat—winning
combine—Accumulate
combine—Collective
comfort zone—Stay
commercial law—Collective
commitment—Act
common ground—Collective
common law—Collective
common sense—Reactive
commonality—Collective
communal law—Collective
communicate—Accept
communicate—Collective
communicate—Conceal
communicate—interaction
communicate—Objective
communicate—Reject
communicate—Reveal
community—Collective
companionship—Collective
compassion—nemonik thinking
compassion—success
compatible—Accept
competence—Reactive
competition—winning
competitions—conventional thinking
complete—nemonik thinking
comply—Accept
comprehension—Collective

comprehension—Objective
comprehension—rational thinking
comprehensive—nemonik thinking
compromise—Accept
compromise—Retreat
compulsion—Reactive
computable—rational thinking
compute—Objective
computer—Objective
computer code—Objective
comradeship—Collective
conceal—Conceal
conceal—interaction
conceal—nemonik
conceal—nemonik thinking
conceal—projection
concede—Accept
concede—Retreat
concentrate—Collective
concentrate—conscious
concentrate—Objective
concentrate—rational thinking
conception—Creative
conciliate—Accept
conclusion—Collective
conclusion—Objective
conclusion—rational thinking
concoct—Conceal
concrete—Objective
concrete—reality
concur—Accept
condemn—Reject
condition—Collective
condition—Reactive
confederate—Collective
confidence—affectorial thinking
confidence—Creative

confidence—projection
confidence—Reactive
confidence—Reveal
confidence—semiconscious
confidence—subconscious
confined—Stay
confirm—Accept
confirmation—Accept
conflict—Collective
conflict—Reject
conflict oriented—conventional thinking
conflict oriented—winning
conform—Accept
conform—Collective
confrontation—winning
Confucius—Collective
confuse—Conceal
conned—Accept
conquer—Accumulate
conquer—Advance
conquest—winning
conscious—Collective
conscious—mind
conscious—nemonik
conscious—nemonik thinking
conscious—Objective
conscious—rational thinking
conscious—thinking
conscious dominance—Collective
conscious dominance—conscious
conscious dominance—Objective
consciousness—Collective
consciousness—mind
consciousness—Objective
consent—Accept
consequence—Collective
consequence—Objective

consequence—Prepare
consequence—rational thinking
conserve—Preserve
consider—Collective
consider—conscious
consider—Objective
consistent—Collective
consistent—Objective
consistent—rational thinking
consistent—Reactive
consolidate—Preserve
consolidate—Stay
consortium—Collective
constant—Objective
constant—Reactive
constrain—Collective
constriction—Retreat
construct—Accumulate
contemplate—Collective
contemplate—Objective
contemplating—rational thinking
contemporary—time
contempt—Reject
contest—winning
contingency—Preserve
contract—Collective
contract—Retreat
contradict—Reject
contribution—Collective
control—Collective
control—conscious
control—Reactive
convergent thinking—conventional thinking
convergent thinking—nemonik thinking
conversation—Accept
conversation—Collective
conversation—Conceal

conversation—interaction
conversation—Reject
conversation—Reveal
conviction—Collective
convince—Collective
convince—Objective
convince—projection
convince—Reveal
convinced—Accept
convincing—rational thinking
cooperate—Collective
coordinate—Prepare
coordinate—Reactive
coordinates—space
copious—Accumulate
correct—Collective
correct—Objective
correct—rational thinking
correct—Reactive
corroborate—Collective
corrupt—Conceal
corrupted—conventional thinking
cosmos—space
counsel—Reveal
countable—Collective
countable—Objective
countable—rational thinking
coup—winning
courage—Act
court of law—Collective
cover-up—Conceal
cowardice—Wait
craving—Reactive
creative—affectorial thinking
creative—Creative
creative—mind
creative—mindmode

creative—nemonik
creative—nemonik thinking
creative—semiconscious
creative—subconscious
creative affecter—Creative
creative mindmode—Creative
creative thinking—conventional thinking
creative thinking—nemonik thinking
creativity—nemonik thinking
criminal—Collective
criminal law—Collective
critical—Collective
critical—Objective
critical—rational thinking
critical—Reveal
critical thinking—conventional thinking
critical thinking—nemonik thinking
critical thinking—nemonik thinking
criticize—Reject
criticizing—conventional thinking
cronies—success
crumble—Retreat
cull—Dispose
cultivate—Accumulate
curator—Preserve
current—time
custodian—Preserve
custody—Stay
customs—Collective
cut loss—Dispose
cut off—Advance
cynical—Collective
cynical—Objective
cynical—projection
cynical—rational thinking
cynical—Reveal

D – KEYWORDS

daring—Act
data—Accept
data—Accumulate
data—Collective
data—Conceal
data—Dispose
data—Objective
data—Preserve
data—rational thinking
data—Reject
data—Reveal
de Bono—Creative
deal breakers—Collective
deal makers—Collective
debate—Collective
debate—interaction
debate—Objective
debate—winning
deceive—Conceal
deceived—Accept
decide—Prepare
decision—Collective
decision—mind
decision—Objective
decision—Reactive
decisive—Act
declare—projection
declare—Reveal
decline—Reject
decline—Retreat
decrease—Retreat
decree—Collective
decry—Reject
deductive—Collective
deductive—Objective

deductive—rational thinking
deductive thinking—conventional thinking
deductive thinking—nemonik thinking
deed—Act
defame—Reject
default—conventional thinking
defeat—Retreat
defeating—conventional thinking
defeating—winning
defect—Retreat
defend—Stay
defragmentation—memory
defragmentation—mind
defragmentation—nemonik
defragmentation—nemonik thinking
defragmentation—subconscious
defragmentation—thinking
defrauded—Accept
degrade—Reject
delay—Stay
delay—Wait
delegate—Prepare
delete—Dispose
deliberate—Collective
deliberate—conscious
deliberate—Objective
deliberate—Reveal
deluded—Accept
delusion—interaction
delusion—Reactive
demeanour—projection
demeanour—Reactive
demeanour—Reveal
demise—Retreat
demolish—Dispose
demonstrate—Collective
demonstrate—Objective

demonstrate—projection
demonstrate—Reveal
demote—Retreat
denigrate—Reject
denounce—Reject
deny—Reject
depart—Retreat
dependable—Reveal
depot—Preserve
deprivation—Dispose
descend—Retreat
desert—Retreat
deserter—Collective
design—Creative
destroy—Dispose
detach—Dispose
detached—conventional thinking
detached—Objective
details—Accept
details—Collective
details—Conceal
details—Objective
details—rational thinking
details—Reject
details—Reveal
detain—Stay
detect—perception
detectable—reality
determination—Reactive
deterministic—Collective
deterministic—Objective
deterministic—rational thinking
deterministic—Reactive
develop—Accumulate
develop—Advance
develop—Creative
devote—Accept

devotion—Reactive
dexterity—Reactive
diagnose—Accept
diagnose—Collective
diagnose—Objective
diagnose—Prepare
diagnose—rational thinking
diagnose—Reject
dialectic—Advance
dialectic—Collective
dialectic—Objective
dialectic—rational thinking
different—Creative
different—Reject
diminish—Dispose
diminish—Retreat
diplomacy—interaction
direction—Prepare
disaccord—Reject
disagreement—Collective
disagreement—Reject
disagreement—winning
disallow—Reject
disappear—Retreat
disapprove—Reject
disbelieve—Collective
disbelieve—Objective
disbelieve—rational thinking
disbelieve—Reject
discard—Dispose
discard—Reject
discern—perception
discipline—Collective
disclose—Reveal
disconnect—Retreat
discontent—Reject
discord—Reject

discount—Reject
discourse—Collective
discourse—interaction
discourse—Objective
discover—Advance
discover—Creative
discriminate—Collective
discriminate—Dispose
discussion—Collective
discussion—interaction
discussion—Objective
disengage—Retreat
disgruntled—Reject
disguise—Conceal
dishonest—Conceal
disinclined—Reject
disinform—Conceal
disintegrate—Retreat
dislike—Reject
disloyal—Conceal
dismantle—Dispose
dismiss—Reject
disorder (chaos)—Creative
disparage—Reject
dispassion—Collective
dispassion—Objective
dispassion—rational thinking
dispassionate—Objective
disperse—Dispose
display—Reveal
displeased—Reject
dispose—Dispose
dispose—matter
dispose—nemonik
dispose—nemonik thinking
dispose—reality
disprove—Reject

dispute—Reject
dispute—winning
disregard—Reject
dissent—Collective
dissent—Reject
dissipate—Dispose
dissociate—Retreat
dissolution—Retreat
distance—space
distaste—Reject
distribute—Dispose
distrust—Collective
distrust—Conceal
distrust—Objective
distrust—rational thinking
distrust—Reject
divergent—Creative
divergent thinking—conventional thinking
divergent thinking—nemonik thinking
divide—Dispose
divorce—Dispose
divorce—Retreat
divulge—Reveal
do—Act
docile—Accept
doctrines—Collective
dogged—Act
dogma—Collective
dogmatic—Reactive
domestic pollution—conventional thinking
double-crossed—Accept
double-deal—Conceal
doubt—Collective
doubt—Conceal
doubt—Objective
doubt—rational thinking
doubt—Reject

downfall—Retreat
downgrade—Retreat
doze—affectorial thinking
doze—Creative
doze—Reactive
doze—semiconscious
doze—subconscious
drill—Collective
drill—Prepare
drill—Reactive
drive—Reactive
dubious—Reject
duped—Accept
duplicity—Conceal
duration—time
duty—Collective
dwindle—Retreat
dwindling resources—conventional thinking
dynamic—Accept
dynamic—Creative
dynamic—nemonik thinking
dynamic thinking—nemonik thinking

E – KEYWORDS

earlier—time
early warning—perception
earn—Accumulate
easy to fool—Accept
eccentric—Creative
educate—Accumulate
educate—Collective
educate—Reveal
educated—conventional thinking
educational system—conventional thinking
efficient—Act
efficient—affectorial thinking
efficient—Collective
efficient—nemonik thinking
efficient—Objective
efficient—rational thinking
efficient—Reactive
effort—Collective
effort—conscious
effort—Objective
effortless—Creative
effortless—rational thinking
effortless—Reactive
ego—mind
ego—Reactive
egoism—Reactive
eject—Dispose
elevation—space
eliminate—Dispose
embed—Stay
embrace—Accept
emergency—Reactive
emotion—Reactive
emotional thinking—conventional thinking
emotional thinking—nemonik thinking

emotionless—Collective
emotionless—Objective
emotionless—rational thinking
emotions—nemonik thinking
empathy—Accept
empirical—Objective
employ—Accumulate
empty mind—affectorial thinking
empty mind—Creative
empty mind—Reactive
empty mind—semiconscious
empty mind—subconscious
encourage—Prepare
encourage—projection
encourage—Reveal
endeavour—Prepare
endorse—Accept
endow—Dispose
enemies—winning
energy—Accumulate
energy—Dispose
energy—matter
energy—Preserve
enforce—Collective
enhance—Accumulate
enlarge—Accumulate
enlighten—Reveal
enquiry—Collective
enquiry—Objective
enquiry—Prepare
enquiry—rational thinking
enrich—Accumulate
ensnare—Conceal
ensnared—Accept
entangled—Accept
enterprise—Prepare
entice—Conceal

entrap—Conceal
entrapped—Accept
entrench—Stay
equilibrium sense—perception
equip—Prepare
equipment—Accumulate
equipment—Dispose
equipment—matter
equipment—Preserve
eradicate—Dispose
erasure—Dispose
erosion—Preserve
escape—Retreat
escape—success
esprit de corps—Collective
esteem—Collective
esteem—projection
esteem—Reveal
estimate—Prepare
eternal—Objective
eternal—time
eternal truth—Objective
eternal truth—rational thinking
ethics—Collective
evacuate—Retreat
evade—Conceal
evade—Retreat
evaluate—Collective
evaluate—Objective
evaluate—Prepare
evaluate—rational thinking
everlasting—time
every possibility—nemonik thinking
evict—Dispose
evidence—Collective
evidence—Objective
evidence—rational thinking

evolve—Creative
exact—Objective
exact—rational thinking
examine—Collective
examine—Objective
examine—perception
examine—rational thinking
excellence—nemonik thinking
except—Reject
exceptional—Creative
excess—Accumulate
exchange—Collective
exchange—interaction
exclude—Dispose
exclude—Reject
execute—Act
exercise—Collective
exercise—conscious
exercise—memory
exercise—Objective
exercise—Prepare
exercise—Reactive
exercise—subconscious
exhaustive—nemonik
exhaustive—nemonik thinking
exhibit—Reveal
exile—Dispose
exit—Retreat
exodus—Retreat
expand—Accumulate
expand—Advance
expand—Creative
expect—mind
expectation—Collective
expectation—Objective
expectation—Reactive
experience—Reactive

experiment—Objective
expert—Collective
expert—Reactive
explain—projection
explain—Reveal
explore—Advance
explore—Creative
explore—perception
expose—Reveal
express—projection
express—Reveal
expulse—Dispose
extend—Accumulate
extend—Advance
extend—Creative
extend—rational thinking
exterior—reality
exterminate—Dispose
external—reality
extinguish—Dispose
extradite—Dispose
extrapolate—Advance
extrapolate—Creative
extrapolate—rational thinking
extravagant—Accumulate
eye contact—interaction
eye contact—projection
eye contact—Reactive
eye contact—Reveal

F – KEYWORDS

fabricate—Conceal
face loss—Collective
face saving—Collective
facial expression—interaction
facial expression—projection
facial expression—Reactive
facial expression—Reveal
facilitate—Accept
facts—Accept
facts—Accumulate
facts—Collective
facts—Conceal
facts—Dispose
facts—Objective
facts—Preserve
facts—rational thinking
facts—Reject
facts—Reveal
factual—rational thinking
fade—Retreat
fail—Retreat
failing—conventional thinking
fairness—Collective
faith—Reactive
fall-back—Retreat
familiar—Reactive
family—Collective
famine—Dispose
fantasy—Creative
fashionable—Collective
fast—Collective
fast—Reactive
fatigued—Accept
feat—success
federation—Collective

feel—perception
feelings—Reactive
feign—Conceal
fiction—Creative
fiction—interaction
fiddled—Accept
fight—winning
figures—Accept
figures—Accumulate
figures—Collective
figures—Conceal
figures—Dispose
figures—Objective
figures—Preserve
figures—rational thinking
figures—Reject
figures—Reveal
finance—Prepare
fire—Dispose
firm—projection
five senses—perception
fix—Preserve
fixed—Stay
flawless—Reactive
flee—Retreat
fleeced—Accept
flexible—Accept
flowing—time
fluid—Accumulate
fluid—Dispose
fluid—matter
fluid—Preserve
focus—Collective
focus—conscious
focus—Objective
focus—rational thinking
foes—winning

folks wisdom—Reactive
follow—Accept
follow—Collective
followers—success
follow-up—Prepare
fooled—Accept
forage—Accumulate
forbid—Reject
force—Accumulate
force—Advance
force—Collective
force—Dispose
force—matter
force—Preserve
forecast—Collective
forecast—Objective
forecast—Prepare
foreseeable—mind
foresight—mind
forever—Objective
forever—time
forfeiture—Retreat
forge ahead—Advance
form—matter
formal—Collective
formal logic—Collective
formal logic—Objective
formal logic—rational thinking
former—time
forsake—Retreat
fortify—Stay
fortune—Accumulate
fortune—Collective
fortune—Dispose
fortune—matter
fortune—Preserve
forward—Advance

foster—Accumulate
fragment ate—Dispose
frank—Reveal
fraternize—Collective
fraud—Conceal
free association—Creative
friends—Accept
friends—Accumulate
friends—Collective
friends—Dispose
friends—matter
friends—Preserve
friends—success
frozen—Stay
frugal—Preserve
fulfilment—success
funds—Accumulate
funds—Collective
funds—Dispose
funds—matter
funds   Preserve
fuse—Collective
future—time

G – KEYWORDS

gain—Accumulate
gas—Accumulate
gas—Dispose
gas—matter
gas—Preserve
gather—Accumulate
generalization—Objective
generate—Creative
generous—Accept
generous—Dispose
genius—Creative
genius—Reactive
genius—subconscious
gestation—Creative
gesticulation—Collective
gesticulation—projection
gesticulation—Reveal
gestures—Collective
gestures—projection
gestures—Reveal
get—Act
get rid of—Dispose
gifted—Creative
gifted—Reactive
gifted—subconscious
give—Dispose
give up—Retreat
give-and-take—Collective
glee—winning
gloat—winning
go—Act
go into—Advance
goad—Conceal
go-ahead—Accept
goal oriented—nemonik thinking

goal oriented—success
goal setting—Prepare
go-getter—Act
goods—Accumulate
goods—Dispose
goods—matter
goods—Preserve
government—Collective
grab—Accumulate
grant—Accept
grant—Dispose
grasp—Accumulate
greed—Accumulate
ground-breaking—Creative
groundskeeper—Preserve
group—Collective
groupthink—Collective
grow—Accumulate
grow—Creative
guardian—Preserve
Guilford—Creative
gullible—Accept
gustatory—reality
gustatory sense—perception
gut feeling—Reactive

H – KEYWORDS

habituation—Collective
habituation—Reactive
half-truth—Conceal
hallucinated—Accept
hallucination—perception
hallucination—Reactive
halt—Stay
happiness—success
hardness—matter
haste—Act
hatching—Creative
headway—Advance
heal—Preserve
healthcare—Collective
hear—perception
hear—reality
Hegel, F.—Objective
Hegel, F.—rational thinking
height—matter
helpers—success
here—space
heretical—Creative
hesitant—Wait
heuristics—Reactive
hidden—Conceal
hidden—Creative
hidden—Reactive
hidden—subconscious
hide—Conceal
hideaway—Preserve
hideout—Preserve
hierarchy—Collective
hierarchy—Prepare
hinder—Reject
hire—Accumulate

history—time
hoard—Accumulate
hoax—Conceal
hold—Preserve
homicide—Dispose
honest—Reveal
honour—Collective
honourable—Reveal
hoodwink—Conceal
hostility—Collective
hunch—Reactive
hunt—Accumulate
hunt—Advance
hustled—Accept
hypnosis—Creative
hypnosis—Reactive
hypnosis—semiconscious
hypnosis—subconscious
hypothesis—Collective
hypothesis—Objective
hypothetical—Collective
hypothetical—mind
hypothetical—Objective

I – KEYWORDS

I—mind
I—Reactive
idea—Creative
identity—mind
identity—Reactive
idle—Stay
idle—subconscious
idle—Wait
if-then arguments—Collective
if-then arguments—Objective
if-then arguments—rational thinking
ignore—Reject
ill-defined—conventional thinking
illogical—affectorial thinking
illogical—Creative
illogical—Reactive
illusion—interaction
illusion—Reactive
illustrate—projection
illustrate—Reveal
image—projection
image—Reveal
imaginary—Accept
imagination—Creative
immaterial—mind
immediately—time
imminent—time
immobile—Stay
impartial—Collective
impartial—Objective
impartial—rational thinking
impartial—reality
impassive—Accept
impatient—Act
impatient—Reactive

impending—time
impersonal—Collective
impersonal—Objective
impersonal—rational thinking
impetuous—Act
implore—projection
implore—Reveal
impose—Collective
impulse—Reactive
impulsive—Act
inaccessible—Creative
inaccessible—Reactive
inaccessible—subconscious
inactive—Creative
inactive—Reactive
inactive—Stay
inactive—subconscious
inactive—Wait
incarcerated—Stay
incautious—Act
inception—Creative
inclination—Reactive
incompatibility—Dispose
incomplete—conventional thinking
incorporate—Accumulate
incorporate—Collective
increase—Accumulate
incubation—Creative
incursion—Advance
indecisive—Wait
independent—Objective
individual—affectorial thinking
individual—mind
individual—Reactive
individual—subconscious
indoctrinate—Collective
inductive—rational thinking

inductive reason—Collective
inductive reason—Objective
inductive thinking—conventional thinking
inductive thinking—nemonik thinking
indulgent—Accept
industrial pollution—conventional thinking
industrial revolution—Objective
inequality—Collective
inert—Stay
inert—subconscious
inert—Wait
inexperience—Creative
inexperienced—Accept
inference—Collective
inference—Objective
inference—rational thinking
infiltrate—Advance
infinite—space
inflexible—Reactive
inflexible—Reject
inflexible—Stay
influence—Collective
influence—Conceal
influence—interaction
influence—mind
influence—nemonik thinking
influence—perception
influence—projection
influence—Reveal
inform—Reveal
informal logic—Reactive
information—Accumulate
information—Conceal
information—Dispose
information—interaction
information—matter
information—nemonik thinking

information—perception
information—Preserve
information—projection
information—Reveal
information management—interaction
information overload—mind
informational revolution—Objective
infrastructure—Collective
infringe—Advance
ingenious—Creative
ingrained—Stay
inhibit—Reject
inhibit conscious—semiconscious
initiative—Act
initiative—Advance
injunction—Reject
injustice—Collective
inner self—mind
inner self—Reactive
innocent—Accept
innocent—Collective
innovation—Creative
inoperative—Stay
inoperative—subconscious
inoperative—Wait
inorganic—matter
inquest—Collective
inquire—perception
inquiry—rational thinking
insanity—mind
insecure—Wait
insight—affectorial thinking
insight—Reactive
insincere—Conceal
insist—projection
insist—Reveal
inspect—perception

inspiration—Creative
inspire—Creative
inspire—Prepare
inspire—projection
inspire—Reveal
instantly—time
instigate—Prepare
instinct—Reactive
institution—Collective
instruct—Reveal
insufficiency—Dispose
insurance—Collective
insurgent—Collective
integrate—Collective
intellect—mind
intelligent—subconscious
interactive—reality
intercept—Advance
interchange—interaction
interdict—Reject
interest—perception
interfere—Act
interim—Wait
interlude—Wait
intermezzo—Wait
interminable—time
intermission—Wait
internalization—Reactive
internalize—Collective
internalize—Reactive
internalize—semiconscious
internalize—subconscious
internet—interaction
interpolate—Collective
interpolate—Objective
interpolate—rational thinking
interpret—Objective

interrupt—Wait
interval—time
interval—Wait
intimidate—Collective
intimidate—projection
intimidate—Reveal
intransigent—Reject
introspection—mind
intrude—Advance
intuition—Reactive
intuitions—nemonik thinking
intuitive thinking—conventional thinking
intuitive thinking—nemonik thinking
intuitive thinking—Reactive
invade—Advance
invention—Creative
invest—Accumulate
investigate—Collective
investigate—Objective
investigate—perception
investigate—Prepare
investigate—rational thinking
involuntarily—Reactive
irrational—affectorial thinking
irrational—Creative
irrational—Reactive
irreconcilable—Dispose
irrefutable—Act
irresolute—Wait

J – KEYWORDS

join—Accumulate
join forces—Collective
joint-venture—Collective
judge—Collective
judgement—Collective
judgement—Objective
judgement—Prepare
judgement—rational thinking
judiciary—Collective
judicious—Preserve

K – KEYWORDS

katas—Reactive
keep up—Preserve
keeper—Preserve
killing—Dispose
kind—Accept
kinetic—reality
kinetic sense—perception
know—conscious
know-how—Collective
know-how—Objective
know-how—Prepare
knowledge—Accumulate
knowledge—Advance
knowledge—Collective
knowledge—Dispose
knowledge—matter
knowledge—memory
knowledge—Objective
knowledge—Prepare
knowledge—Preserve
knowledge—rational thinking
knowledge—Reactive
knowledge—Reveal
known territory—Retreat

L – KEYWORDS

lack—Dispose
landslide—winning
language—Accept
language—Collective
language—interaction
language—Prepare
language—Reveal
Lao Zi—Collective
Lao Zi—nemonik thinking
Lao Zi—Objective
Lao Zi—Reactive
Lao Zi—success
later—time
lateral thinking—conventional thinking
lateral thinking—Creative
lateral thinking—nemonik thinking
latitude—space
lavish—Accumulate
law and order—Collective
law enforcement—Collective
law of causality—Collective
law of causality—Objective
law of causality—rational thinking
law-making—Collective
laws—Collective
laws—Objective
laws—rational thinking
lawyer—Collective
lax—Accept
lay off—Dispose
lazy—Wait
leader—Collective
leadership—Collective
leadership—Prepare
league—Collective

leak—Reveal
learn—Accumulate
learn—Collective
learn—conscious
learn—memory
learn—mind
learn—Objective
learn—perception
learn—Prepare
learn—Reactive
learn—subconscious
lease—Accumulate
least effort—Collective
least effort—Objective
least effort—rational thinking
least effort—Reactive
least resistance—Collective
least resistance—Objective
least resistance—rational thinking
least resistance—Reactive
leave—Retreat
lecture—projection
lecture—Reveal
legalize—Collective
length—matter
lethargic—Stay
lethargic—Wait
letters—Collective
letters—interaction
letters—Reveal
level-headed—Objective
level-headed—rational thinking
liaise—Collective
lie—Conceal
lifeless—Stay
limitless—space
linear—time

linear thinking—conventional thinking
linear thinking—nemonik thinking
listen—perception
literature review—Objective
loathing—Reject
location—space
logic—Accumulate
logic—Advance
logic—Collective
logic—Objective
logic—rational thinking
logical thinking—conventional thinking
logical thinking—nemonik thinking
logistics—matter
lonely—Dispose
longitude—space
look after—Preserve
loose collection—conventional thinking
lose—Dispose
lose—Retreat
love—Collective
loyal—Reveal
lull—Wait
lure—Conceal
lured—Accept
luxury—Accumulate

M – KEYWORDS

machinery—Accumulate
machinery—Dispose
machinery—matter
machinery—Preserve
magistrate—Collective
magnitude—matter
maintain—Preserve
make—Accumulate
make-believe—Conceal
making rules—Collective
malfunction—Stay
malleable—Accept
mana—Collective
mana—projection
mana—Reactive
mana—Reveal
management—Collective
management—Prepare
manifest—conscious
manipulate—Collective
manipulate—Conceal
manmade—Collective
mannerisms—Collective
mannerisms—projection
mannerisms—Reactive
mannerisms—Reveal
manoeuvre—Prepare
manslaughter—Dispose
manufacture—Accumulate
manufacture—Collective
marketing—Prepare
mask—Conceal
mass—matter
massacre—Dispose
match—winning

material—Accumulate
material—Dispose
material—matter
material—Preserve
material—reality
material body—reality
mathematics—Objective
matter—Accumulate
matter—Dispose
matter—Preserve
maturation—Reactive
maximize—Collective
maximize—Objective
maximize—rational thinking
maximize—Reactive
maxims—Reactive
me—mind
me—Reactive
measureable—rational thinking
measurement—Objective
mediate—Accept
mediate—Collective
meditation—affectorial thinking
meditation—Creative
meditation—Reactive
meditation—semiconscious
meditation—subconscious
memorize—Accumulate
memory—mind
memory—nemonik thinking
memory—Reactive
memory—semiconscious
memory—subconscious
memory pegs—memory
memory pegs—nemonik
memory pegs—nemonik thinking
mend—Preserve

mental—mind
mental checklist—memory
mental checklist—nemonik
mental checklist—nemonik thinking
mental habituation—Reactive
mental illness—mind
mental layers—mind
mental model—Collective
mental model—Creative
mental model—Objective
mental model—Reactive
mental network—memory
mental network—nemonik
mental network—nemonik thinking
mental perfection—Reactive
mental process—Collective
mental process—Creative
mental process—memory
mental process—nemonik thinking
mental process—Objective
mental process—Reactive
mental process—thinking
mental prompts—affectorial thinking
mental reorganization—nemonik
mental reorganization—nemonik thinking
mental reorganization—Reactive
mental reorganization—subconscious
mental signals—affecters
mental signals—affectorial thinking
mental signals—mind
mental signals—nemonik
mental signals—subconscious
mental state—conscious
mental state—mind
mental state—semiconscious
mental state—subconscious
mentalism—mind

mentality—mind
mentation—mind
merge—Accumulate
messages—Collective
messages—interaction
messages—Reveal
meta-thinking—nemonik thinking
methodical—Collective
methodical—Objective
methodical—rational thinking
methodical—Reactive
meticulous—Collective
meticulous—Objective
mettle—Act
military—Collective
mind—affectorial thinking
mind—Collective
mind—conscious
mind—Creative
mind—memory
mind—nemonik
mind—nemonik thinking
mind—Objective
mind—rational thinking
mind—Reactive
mind—semiconscious
mind—subconscious
mind—thinking
mind control—Reactive
mind management—affectorial thinking
mind management—mind
mind management—nemonik
mind management—nemonik thinking
mind management—Reactive
mind management—semiconscious
mind management—subconscious
minder—Preserve

minding—Preserve
mindmode—mind
mindpower—Reactive
mindpower—subconscious
mindset—Reactive
mindware—mind
mindware—nemonik
mindware—nemonik thinking
mindware—Reactive
minerals—Accumulate
minerals—Dispose
minerals—matter
minerals—Preserve
minimum effort—Collective
minimum effort—Objective
minimum effort—rational thinking
minimum effort—Reactive
misinform—Conceal
mislead—Conceal
misled—Accept
misrepresent—Conceal
mission—Prepare
mission—success
mistrust—Collective
mistrust—Conceal
mistrust—Objective
mistrust—rational thinking
mistrust—Reactive
mistrust—Reject
mnemonic—memory
mnemonic—nemonik
mnemonic—nemonik thinking
mnemonic—Reactive
mnemonic—subconscious
mobile—space
model of the mind—nemonik
model of the mind—nemonik thinking

moderate—Accept
modern—time
modifiable—Collective
mole—perception
mollify—Accept
moment—time
momentum—Advance
momentum—Retreat
momentum—space
money—Accumulate
money—Collective
money—Dispose
money—matter
money—Preserve
morals—Collective
motion—space
motionless—Stay
motivate—Collective
motivate—Prepare
motivate—projection
motivate—Reactive
motivate—Reveal
mottos—Collective
move ahead—Advance
movement—space
multiple solutions—Creative
murder—Dispose
mutable—Collective
mutiny—Collective
mutiny—Dispose
mutual support—Collective
myself—mind
myself—Reactive
mystery—subconscious

N – KEYWORDS

naive—Accept
napping—affectorial thinking
napping—Creative
napping—Reactive
napping—semiconscious
napping—subconscious
narrow-minded—Reject
nation—Collective
natural—Objective
need—nemonik thinking
need—success
negative reinforcement—Collective
negotiate—Collective
nemeses—winning
nemonik accelerator—Collective
nemonik accelerator—conscious
nemonik accelerator—Creative
nemonik accelerator—mind
nemonik accelerator—nemonik thinking
nemonik accelerator—Objective
nemonik accelerator—rational thinking
nemonik thinking—Accept
nemonik thinking—Accumulate
nemonik thinking—Act
nemonik thinking—Advance
nemonik thinking—affectorial thinking
nemonik thinking—Collective
nemonik thinking—Conceal
nemonik thinking—conscious
nemonik thinking—Creative
nemonik thinking—Dispose
nemonik thinking—interaction
nemonik thinking—matter
nemonik thinking—mind
nemonik thinking—Objective

nemonik thinking—perception
nemonik thinking—Prepare
nemonik thinking—Preserve
nemonik thinking—projection
nemonik thinking—rational thinking
nemonik thinking—Reactive
nemonik thinking—reality
nemonik thinking—Reject
nemonik thinking—Retreat
nemonik thinking—Reveal
nemonik thinking—semiconscious
nemonik thinking—space
nemonik thinking—Stay
nemonik thinking—subconscious
nemonik thinking—time
nemonik thinking—Wait
nemoniks—Creative
nerve—Act
network—Collective
network—Prepare
neural plasticity—memory
neural plasticity—mind
neural plasticity—nemonik
neural plasticity—nemonik thinking
neural plasticity—Reactive
neural plasticity—subconscious
neural plasticity—thinking
neutral—Objective
neutral—rational thinking
never-ending—time
new—Creative
news media—Accept
news media—interaction
Newtonian reality—reality
next—time
nip in the bud—Act
non-assertive—Accept

non-assertive—Conceal
non-assertive—Dispose
non-assertive—perception
non-assertive—Retreat
non-assertive—Wait
nonconforming—Collective
non-critical—Accept
non-critical—Creative
non-critical—perception
non-critical—Reactive
non-judgmental—Accept
non-judgmental—Creative
non-judgmental—perception
non-judgmental—Reactive
non-living—matter
nonmaterial—mind
nonmaterial—space
nonmaterial—time
non-verbal—interaction
non-verbal—perception
non-verbal—projection
normal—reality
noticeable—perception
notion—Creative
novel—Creative
now—time
numbers—Accept
numbers—Accumulate
numbers—Collective
numbers—Conceal
numbers—Dispose
numbers—Objective
numbers—Preserve
numbers—rational thinking
numbers—Reject
numbers—Reveal
nurture—Accumulate

O – KEYWORDS

obey—Accept
objection—Reject
objective—conscious
objective—mind
objective—mindmode
objective—nemonik
objective—nemonik thinking
objective—Objective
objective—rational thinking
objective truth—Objective
obligation—Collective
obliterate—Dispose
oblivious—Creative
oblivious—Reactive
oblivious—subconscious
obscure—Conceal
obscure—Creative
obscured—subconscious
observation—Objective
observe—perception
obsolete—Dispose
obstinate—Reject
obstruct—Conceal
obtain—Accumulate
obtain—nemonik thinking
obtain—success
occupy—Accumulate
Ockham's razor—Collective
Ockham's razor—Objective
Ockham's razor—rational thinking
offensive—Advance
officials—Collective
offload—Dispose
old—time
olfactory—reality

olfactory sense—perception
omit—Reject
one-dimensional—time
open—Reveal
open mind—mind
open mind—Reactive
operating system—mind
operating system—nemonik
operating system—nemonik thinking
operation—Prepare
opponents—conventional thinking
opponents—winning
opportunism—Act
opportunity—Creative
opposition—Collective
opposition—Reject
oppress—Collective
optimization—Reactive
optimize—nemonik thinking
option—mind
opulence—Accumulate
order—Collective
order—Objective
order—rational thinking
order—Reactive
organic—matter
organize—affectorial thinking
organize—Collective
organize—conscious
organize—mind
organize—nemonik thinking
organize—Objective
organize—Prepare
organize—rational thinking
organize—Reactive
organize—subconscious
original—Creative

ostracise—Collective
ostracise—Dispose
ostracise—Reject
out of action—Stay
out of order—Stay
outcast—Collective
outcast—Dispose
outcast—Reject
outdated—Dispose
outflank—Advance
outflank—space
outflanked—Retreat
outlaw—Collective
outlaw—Reject
outmanoeuvre—space
outrun—Advance
outrun—Retreat
outrun—space
overhaul—Preserve
overload protection—Reactive
overload protection—subconscious
overpopulation—conventional thinking
overrule—Collective
overrule—Reject
overrun—Advance
overrun—Retreat
overrun—space
oversupply—Accumulate
oversupply—Dispose
overt—Conceal
overthrow—Accumulate
overthrow—Advance
overthrow—Collective
overthrow—space
overthrow—winning
overwhelm—Accumulate
overwhelm—Advance

overwhelm—Collective
overwhelm—space
ownership—Accumulate

P – KEYWORDS

pacify—Accept
pacify—Collective
pacify—Reveal
pact—Collective
panic—Act
paralysed—Stay
paralysis—Wait
paranoid—Conceal
paranoid—Reject
paraphrasing—perception
parliament—Collective
parsimonious—Preserve
parting—Retreat
partners—success
partnership—Collective
passive—Stay
past—time
patience—Wait
pattern—Collective
pattern—Objective
pattern—rational thinking
pause—Stay
pause—Wait
peace—Accept
peaceful—Creative
peaceful—Reactive
peaceful—semiconscious
peaceful—subconscious
peer pressure—Collective
peer review—Objective
penalty—Collective
pending—Wait
penetrate—Advance
pennywise—Preserve
people—Accumulate

people—Collective
people—Dispose
people—matter
people—mind
people—nemonik thinking
people—Preserve
perceive—perception
perceptible—perception
perfection—Collective
perfection—Reactive
perforate—Advance
perform—Act
period—time
permanent—space
permanent—time
permit—Accept
perpetual—space
perpetual—time
persistent—Conceal
persistent—projection
persistent—Reactive
persistent—Reveal
persona—mind
persona—Reactive
personal—affectorial thinking
personal—Reactive
personality—mind
personality—Reactive
persuade—Collective
persuade—projection
persuade—Reveal
physical—mind
physical habituation—Reactive
physical perfection—Reactive
physics—Objective
physiological—mind
pierce—Advance

pig-headed—Reject
pioneer—Advance
pioneer—Creative
placate—Accept
place—space
planning—Prepare
plants—Accumulate
plants—Dispose
plants—matter
plants—Preserve
plead—projection
plead—Reveal
pledge—projection
pledge—Reveal
plenty—Accumulate
pliable—Accept
plunge—Advance
point—space
police—Collective
policies—Collective
polite—projection
polite—Reactive
polite—Reveal
politicians—Collective
politics—Collective
pollution—conventional thinking
poorly understood—conventional thinking
position—space
positioning—Accumulate
positioning—Act
positioning—Advance
positioning—Collective
positioning—Dispose
positioning—Prepare
positioning—Preserve
positioning—Retreat
positioning—Stay

positioning—Wait
positive reinforcement—Collective
possession—Accumulate
postpone—Stay
postpone—Wait
posture—projection
posture—Reactive
posture—Reveal
pounce—Advance
poverty—Dispose
power—Collective
power—matter
practical—rational thinking
practice—Accumulate
practice—Prepare
practice—Reactive
practise—Prepare
practise—Reactive
pragmatic—Reactive
preceding—time
precise—Collective
precise—Objective
precise—rational thinking
precise—Reactive
preclude—Act
predict—Collective
predict—mind
predict—Objective
predict—Prepare
predict—rational thinking
predict—Reactive
predictable—Reactive
predisposition—Reactive
preference—mind
prejudice—Collective
premature—Act
premise—Collective

premise—Objective
premise—rational thinking
premonition—Reactive
prepare—nemonik
prepare—nemonik thinking
prepare—Prepare
prepare—reality
prepare—time
prerequisites—Prepare
prerogative—Collective
present—projection
present—Reveal
present—time
presentiment—Reactive
preserve—matter
preserve—nemonik
preserve—nemonik thinking
preserve—Preserve
preserve—reality
prestige—Collective
prestige—projection
prestige—Reveal
presumed—mind
pretend—Conceal
prevent—Act
prevent—Reject
previous—time
prior—time
prioritizing—Prepare
privilege—Collective
proactive—Act
probability—rational thinking
probe—Collective
probe—Objective
probe—perception
probe—rational thinking
problem solving—memory

problem solving—mind
problem solving—nemonik
problem solving—nemonik thinking
problem solving—thinking
procedures—Collective
proclaim—projection
proclaim—Reveal
procrastinate—Stay
procrastinate—Wait
procure—Accumulate
prod—Advance
produce—Accumulate
professional—rational thinking
proficiency—Collective
proficiency—Reactive
profit—Accumulate
profit—matter
profuse—Accumulate
prognosis—Prepare
programmed—Reactive
programming—Collective
progress—Accumulate
progress—Advance
progress—Collective
progress—Creative
progress—Objective
progress—Reactive
progressing—time
prohibit—Reject
prolong—Wait
prominence—projection
promise—Accept
promise—projection
promise—Reveal
promote—Advance
promote—Prepare
promote—projection

promote—Reveal
prompt—affectorial thinking
prompt—interaction
prompt—memory
prompt—nemonik
prompt—nemonik thinking
prompt—Reactive
prompt memory—memory
prompt memory—nemonik
prompt memory—nemonik thinking
prompt thinking—nemonik
prompt thinking—nemonik thinking
prompt thinking—thinking
pronounce—projection
pronounce—Reveal
proof—Objective
propaganda—Collective
propagate—Accumulate
propagate—Advance
property—Accumulate
property—Dispose
property—matter
property—Preserve
proscribe—Reject
prosecutor—Collective
prosperity—Accumulate
protect—Preserve
protect—Stay
protocols—Collective
prove—Collective
prove—Objective
prove—projection
prove—Reveal
provoke—Accumulate
provoke—Act
provoke—Advance
provoke—projection

provoke—Reject
provoke—Reveal
prudent—Preserve
psychiatry—mind
psychology—mind
public law—Collective
publicity—Reveal
publish—projection
publish—Reveal
pullback—Retreat
puncture—Advance
punish—Collective
punish—Dispose
punish—Prepare
purchase—Accumulate
purge—Collective
purge—Dispose
purpose—Prepare
pursue—Advance
push—Advance
put on hold—Wait

Q – KEYWORDS

quality—matter
quantifiable—rational thinking
quantity—matter
quarrel—winning
quarrelsome—Reject
question—Collective
question—interaction
question—Objective
question—rational thinking
questioning—nemonik thinking
quick—Collective
quick—Reactive

R – KEYWORDS

raid—Accumulate
raid—Advance
raise—Accumulate
random sampling—Objective
randomization—Creative
rapid—Collective
rapid—Reactive
rash—Act
rash—Reactive
ratify—Accept
ratify—Collective
rational thinking—conventional thinking
rational thinking—nemonik thinking
rationalizing—conventional thinking
raw material—Accumulate
raw material—Dispose
raw material—matter
raw material—Preserve
reaction—Reactive
reactive—affectorial thinking
reactive—mind
reactive—mindmode
reactive—nemonik
reactive—nemonik thinking
reactive—Reactive
reactive—Reveal
reactive—semiconscious
reactive—subconscious
reactive affecter—Reactive
reactive mindmode—Reactive
read—perception
real—reality
real estate—matter
realism—reality
realistic—reality

reality—sensory reality
realization—Creative
realization—success
rear-guard—Retreat
reason—Collective
reason—conventional thinking
reason—nemonik thinking
reason—Objective
reason—rational thinking
reasonable—Collective
reasonable—Objective
reasonable—reality
reassure—projection
reassure—Reveal
rebel—Collective
rebel—Reject
rebut—Reject
recall—Dispose
recall—mind
recall—Retreat
recede—Retreat
recess—Wait
reciprocity—Collective
reckless—Act
reclaim—Preserve
recognition—Accept
recognition—projection
recoil—Retreat
recommend—Accept
reconcile—Accept
reconnaissance—perception
recoup—Preserve
recover—Preserve
recover—Retreat
recover—Stay
recruit—Accumulate
recruits—matter

recuperate—Preserve
recuperate—Retreat
recuperate—Stay
red tape—Collective
reduce—Dispose
reduce—Retreat
redundant—Dispose
reflex—Act
reflex—Reactive
reformulate—Creative
refurbish—Preserve
refuse—Dispose
refuse—Reject
regain—Preserve
regenerate—Preserve
regress—Retreat
regret—Reactive
regroup—Retreat
regulate—Collective
reject—interaction
reject—nemonik
reject—nemonik thinking
reject—perception
reject—Reject
relationship—Collective
relax—affectorial thinking
relax—Creative
relax—projection
relax—Reactive
relax—semiconscious
relax—Stay
relax—subconscious
relax—Wait
release—Dispose
release—Reveal
reliability test—Objective
reliable—Collective

reliable—Objective
reliable—rational thinking
reliable—Reactive
reliable—Reveal
relinquish—Retreat
relocate—Retreat
reluctant—Wait
remember—Accumulate
remember—mind
remember—Reactive
remorse—Reactive
remove—Dispose
renew—Preserve
renovate—Preserve
reorganize—Prepare
reorganize—Retreat
repair—Preserve
repetition—Reactive
repetitive behaviours—Reactive
repetitive thoughts—Reactive
replenish—Preserve
replicable—Objective
repose—Stay
repose—subconscious
repose—Wait
reposition—Retreat
repossess—Preserve
representatives—Collective
repress—Collective
reprieve—Wait
reputation—Collective
reputation—projection
reputation—Reveal
requirements—Prepare
rescue—Preserve
resentment—Collective
resign—Dispose

resign—Retreat
resistance—Collective
resolute—Act
resolution—conscious
resolution—Reactive
resolve—Accept
resolve—Reactive
resource management—matter
resources—Accumulate
resources—Dispose
resources—matter
resources—Preserve
respect—Collective
respect—projection
respect—Reveal
response—Act
responsible—Prepare
responsible—Reveal
responsive—Reactive
rest—affectorial thinking
rest—Creative
rest—Reactive
rest—semiconscious
rest—Stay
rest—subconscious
rest—Wait
restore—Preserve
restrain—Wait
restrict—Retreat
restructure—Retreat
result—Objective
results—rational thinking
retain—Preserve
retention—Preserve
retire—Retreat
retort—Act
retract—Retreat

retreat—nemonik
retreat—nemonik thinking
retreat—reality
retreat—Retreat
retreat—space
retrieve—Preserve
return—Retreat
revamp—Preserve
reveal—interaction
reveal—nemonik
reveal—nemonik thinking
reveal—projection
reveal—Reveal
revenue—Accumulate
revenue—Dispose
revenue—matter
revenue—Preserve
reverse—Retreat
review—Collective
review—Objective
review—Prepare
review—rational thinking
revise—Prepare
revitalize—Preserve
revolt—Collective
reward—Collective
rich—Accumulate
right moment—Wait
righteous—conventional thinking
rights—Collective
rigid—Reactive
rigid—Stay
rip off—Accept
risk avoidance—Prepare
risk avoidance—Reject
risk avoidance—Wait
risk management—Prepare

risk taking—Accept
risk taking—Act
risk taking—Prepare
rivals—winning
rob—Accumulate
robots—Accumulate
robots—Dispose
robots—matter
robots—Preserve
round—winning
roused—Act
roused—conscious
roused—Reactive
rout—Retreat
rout—winning
routine—Reactive
row—winning
rubbish—Dispose
rule of thumb—Reactive
rules—Collective
ruling—Collective
rush—Advance

S – KEYWORDS

safeguard—Preserve
safety—Collective
safety—Wait
salvage—Preserve
samples—Objective
sanction—Reject
sanctuary—Preserve
sanitize—Dispose
sanity—mind
sarcastic—Collective
sarcastic—projection
sarcastic—Reveal
save—Preserve
scarcity—Dispose
scare—Collective
scare—projection
scare—Reveal
SCARRED—conventional thinking
scenario—Prepare
sceptic—Collective
sceptic—Objective
sceptic—rational thinking
sceptic—Reject
scheduling—Prepare
schematic—Collective
schematic—Objective
schematic—Prepare
schematic—rational thinking
scheme—Conceal
science—Objective
scientific thinking—conventional thinking
scientific thinking—nemonik thinking
scientific truth—Objective
scorched earth—Dispose
scorn—Reject

scout—perception
scrap—Dispose
scrutinize—Collective
scrutinize—Objective
scrutinize—perception
scrutinize—Prepare
scrutinize—rational thinking
scuttle—Dispose
sealed—subconscious
search—Advance
search—Collective
search—Creative
search—Objective
search—perception
search—Prepare
secrets—Collective
secrets—Conceal
secure—Preserve
secure—Wait
see—perception
see—reality
seek—nemonik thinking
seek—success
segmentation—Dispose
seize—Accumulate
seize—Advance
self—mind
self—Reactive
self—subconscious
self-assurance—conscious
self-confidence—Reactive
self-conscious—Reactive
self-control—conscious
self-control—Reactive
self-deception—Accept
self-discipline—conscious
self-discipline—Reactive

self-doubt—Reactive
self-hypnosis—Reactive
self-hypnosis—semiconscious
self-hypnosis—subconscious
selfish—Reactive
selfish—Reject
selfless—Accept
selfless—Reactive
self-organizing—memory
self-organizing—mind
self-organizing—nemonik thinking
self-organizing—thinking
semiconscious—mind
semiconscious—subconscious
semiconscious dominance—affectorial thinking
semiconscious dominance—Creative
semiconscious dominance—Reactive
semiconscious dominance—semiconscious
semiconscious dominance—subconscious
send-off—Dispose
sensations—Reactive
senses—perception
senses—sensory reality
sensible—Preserve
sensible—Reactive
sensitive—perception
sensitive—Reveal
sensory—reality
sensory observation—perception
sensory processes—perception
sentence—Collective
sentinel—Stay
sentry—Stay
separate—Dispose
sequential—rational thinking
sequential—time
serenity—Reactive

serenity—semiconscious
set—Stay
set goals—Prepare
set of rules—Reactive
setback—Retreat
settle—Accept
settlement—Collective
setup—Conceal
sham—Conceal
shape—matter
share—Collective
share—Dispose
shed—Dispose
shelter—Collective
shelter—Preserve
shelter—Stay
shortage—Dispose
shorten supply-lines—Retreat
show—projection
show—Reveal
shrink—Retreat
shrivel—Retreat
shunt—Advance
sign—Accept
signals—affectorial thinking
silence—perception
silent mind—affectorial thinking
silent mind—Creative
silent mind—Reactive
silent mind—semiconscious
silent mind—subconscious
single-minded—Reactive
site—space
sixth sense—Reactive
size—matter
skill—Collective
skill—Prepare

skill—Reactive
slack—Wait
slash and burn—Dispose
slaughter—Dispose
sleep—affectorial thinking
sleep—Creative
sleep—Reactive
sleep—semiconscious
sleep—subconscious
slumber—affectorial thinking
slumber—Creative
slumber—Reactive
slumber—semiconscious
slumber—subconscious
smell—perception
smell—reality
smokescreen—Conceal
snare—Conceal
snared—Accept
snatch—Accumulate
snitch—perception
sociable—Collective
social media—interaction
social struggle—Collective
society—Collective
software—rational thinking
solicitor—Collective
solid—matter
solidarity—Accept
solution oriented—perception
soothe—Accept
soul—mind
soul—Reactive
spare—Preserve
spatial—reality
spatial management—space
speak—projection

speak—Reveal
spearhead—Advance
spearhead—Creative
specialist—Collective
specialist—Reactive
speed—Act
speed—Advance
speed—Collective
speed—Reactive
speed—Retreat
speed—space
spendthrift—Dispose
spin—Conceal
spineless—Accept
spirit—mind
spirit—Reactive
split—Dispose
spread—Dispose
spy—perception
squabble—winning
squander—Dispose
squealer—perception
stable—Collective
stable—Reactive
stack—Accumulate
staff—Accumulate
staff—Collective
staff—Dispose
staff—matter
staff—Preserve
stagnant—Reactive
stagnant—Reject
stagnant—Stay
stagnant—Wait
stall—Stay
stall—Wait
stance—Act

stance—Collective
stance—projection
stance—Reveal
stanch—Act
standby—Preserve
standby—Stay
standstill—Stay
stash—Accumulate
state of mind—mind
state-of-the-art—Creative
static—Reactive
static—Reject
static—Stay
static thinking—conventional thinking
stationary—Stay
stationary—Wait
statistical analyses—Objective
statistics—Accumulate
statistics—Collective
statistics—Dispose
statistics—Objective
statistics—Preserve
statistics—rational thinking
status—Collective
status—projection
status—Reveal
status quo—Collective
status quo—Reactive
stay—nemonik
stay—nemonik thinking
stay—reality
stay—space
stay—Stay
steadfast—Act
steady—Act
steal—Accumulate
steward—Preserve

stimulate—Prepare
stimulate—projection
stimulate—Reveal
stingy—Accumulate
stock—Accumulate
stock—Dispose
stock—matter
stock—Preserve
stockpile—Preserve
stockroom—Preserve
storage—Preserve
store—Preserve
storehouse—Preserve
storeroom—Preserve
storm—Advance
straightforward—Reveal
strange—Creative
strategical thinking—conventional thinking
strategical thinking—nemonik
strategical thinking—nemonik thinking
strategical thinking—nemonik thinking
strategical thinking—thinking
strategy—Prepare
strength—matter
strict—Reject
strike—Act
strike—Advance
structural thinking—nemonik
structural thinking—nemonik thinking
structural thinking—thinking
structure—Collective
structure—Objective
structure—Prepare
structure—rational thinking
stubborn—Reactive
study—Accumulate
study—memory

study—Prepare
study—Reactive
subconscious—nemonik thinking
subdivide—Collective
subdivide—Prepare
subjective—affectorial thinking
subjective—Creative
subjective—Reactive
subjugation—winning
submission—Collective
submissive—Accept
submissive—projection
subordinates—Collective
subordinates—Prepare
subside—Retreat
substance—matter
success—nemonik thinking
successive approximation—Collective
successive approximation—Objective
successive approximation—rational thinking
successive approximation—Reactive
succumb—Accept
suggestibility—affectorial thinking
suggestibility—Reactive
suggestibility—Reactive
suggestibility—semiconscious
suggestibility—subconscious
summarize—Collective
summarize—Objective
summarize—perception
summarize—Prepare
supervise—Collective
supervise—Prepare
supplies—Accumulate
supplies—Dispose
supplies—matter
supplies—Prepare

supplies—Preserve
supply—matter
supply lines—Advance
supply lines—matter
supply lines—Retreat
supply lines—Stay
support—Accept
support—Accumulate
support—Collective
support—Preserve
support—projection
support—Reveal
supporters—success
supportive results—Objective
suppress—Collective
sure—Act
surface—matter
surpass—Advance
surplus—Accumulate
surprise—Advance
surprise—Conceal
surprising—Creative
surrender—Accept
surrender—Retreat
surround—Advance
surveillance—perception
survival—nemonik thinking
survival—Retreat
survival—success
suspend—Wait
suspicious—Collective
suspicious—Objective
suspicious—rational thinking
suspicious—Reject
sustain—Preserve
sway—Collective
sway—Conceal

sway—projection
sway—Reactive
sway—Reveal
swear—Collective
swear—projection
swear—Reveal
swift—Collective
swift—Reactive
swindled—Accept
swoop—Advance
SWOT—Prepare
SWOT-analysis—nemonik thinking
sympathetic—Accept
synchronize—Prepare
syndicate—Collective
synthesis—Objective
synthesis—rational thinking
synthesize—Prepare
systematic—Collective
systematic—nemonik thinking
systematic—Objective
systematic—rational thinking
systematic—Reactive
systematic thinking—nemonik
systematic thinking—nemonik thinking
systematic thinking—thinking

T – KEYWORDS

tackle—Act
tact—Conceal
tact—projection
tact—Reveal
tactical thinking—conventional thinking
tactical thinking—nemonik
tactical thinking—nemonik thinking
tactical thinking—thinking
tactics—Prepare
tactile—reality
tactile sense—perception
take—Accumulate
takeover—Accumulate
takeover—winning
talent—Creative
talent—mind
talent—Reactive
talent—subconscious
talk—projection
talk—Reveal
target—Prepare
task setting—Prepare
taste—perception
taste—reality
teach—Reveal
teachable—nemonik
teachable—nemonik thinking
team—Collective
team spirit—Collective
team up—Collective
teamwork—Collective
tell—Reveal
temporal—reality
temporal—time
temporary—Collective

tempt—Conceal
tend—Preserve
terminate—Dispose
terror—Collective
terror—projection
terror—Reveal
test—Objective
that—matter
theoretical construct—mind
theory—Objective
there—space
thermal—reality
thermal sense—perception
thesis—Collective
thesis—Creative
thesis—Objective
thesis—rational thinking
thickness—matter
this—matter
thought—mind
threat—Accumulate
threat—Act
threat—Advance
threat—Conceal
threat—projection
threat—Reject
three-dimensional—matter
three-dimensional—space
thrifty—Preserve
throw away—Dispose
thrust—Advance
thrust—matter
thrust aside—Dispose
tight-fisted—Accumulate
time management—time
time off—Wait
timeless—time

timely—time
time-out—affectorial thinking
time-out—Creative
time-out—Reactive
time-out—Stay
time-out—subconscious
time-out—time
timing—time
today—time
together—Collective
tolerate—Accept
tomorrow—time
tools—Accumulate
tools—Dispose
tools—matter
tools—Preserve
torment—projection
torment—Reveal
touch—perception
touch—reality
trade—Accumulate
trailblazer—Creative
train—affectorial thinking
train—Collective
train—conscious
train—Creative
train—memory
train—Objective
train—Reactive
train—subconscious
train—thinking
training—Prepare
training—Reactive
traitor—Collective
traits—mind
traits—Reactive
trajectory—space

tranquil—semiconscious
tranquillity—Creative
tranquillity—Reactive
tranquillity—subconscious
transfer—Prepare
transfer—space
transform—matter
transmit—projection
transport—matter
transport—space
trap—Conceal
trap—projection
trapped—Accept
trash—Dispose
travel—space
treasure—Accumulate
treasure—Dispose
treasure—matter
treasure—Preserve
treaty—Accept
treaty—Collective
trial—Collective
tribe—Collective
tribunal—Collective
trick—Conceal
tricked—Accept
triumph—winning
truce—Accept
trust—Accept
trust—Reactive
trust—Reveal
trustworthy—Reveal
truth—Collective
truth—Objective
truth—rational thinking
truth—Reactive
turmoil—Creative

turnaround—Retreat
tutor—Reveal
twilight state—affectorial thinking
twilight state—Creative
twilight state—Reactive
twilight state—semiconscious
twilight state—subconscious
tyrannize—Collective

U – KEYWORDS

unambiguous—Objective
unambiguous—projection
unaware—Creative
unaware—Reactive
unaware—subconscious
unbending—Act
unbiased—Objective
unbiased—rational thinking
unchanging—Objective
unchanging—Reactive
unchanging—Stay
uncommitted—Wait
unconfident—Wait
unconventional—Creative
unconvinced—Reject
uncover—Creative
uncover—Objective
uncover—rational thinking
uncritical—Accept
uncritical—affectorial thinking
uncritical—Creative
uncritical—Reactive
undependable—Conceal
understanding—Collective
understanding—Objective
understanding—rational thinking
undertaking—Prepare
unemotional—Collective
unemotional—conscious
unemotional—Objective
unemotional—projection
unemotional—rational thinking
unending—time
unessential—Dispose
unexpected—Advance

unexpected—Creative
unfair—Collective
unfaithful—Conceal
unfamiliar—Creative
unfamiliar—Wait
unify—Accept
unify—Collective
unimpressed—Reject
uninterested—Reject
unique—Creative
unite—Accumulate
unite—Collective
universe—space
unknown—affectorial thinking
unknown—Creative
unknown—Reactive
unknown—subconscious
unknown territory—Advance
unmoved—Reject
unmoving—Stay
unnatural—Collective
unorthodox—Creative
unplanned—affectorial thinking
unplanned—Creative
unpredictable—affectorial thinking
unpredictable—Creative
unprejudiced—Objective
unproductive—Wait
unproven—affectorial thinking
unproven—Creative
unquestioning—Accept
unreasonable—affectorial thinking
unreasonable—Creative
unreasonable—Reactive
unreliable—Conceal
unresolved—Reject
unselfish—Accept

unsubstantial—mind
unsubstantial—space
unsubstantial—time
unsubstantiated—affectorial thinking
unsubstantiated—Creative
unsubstantiated—Reactive
unsure—Wait
unsuspecting—Accept
unsympathetic—Reject
unsystematic—affectorial thinking
unsystematic—conventional thinking
unsystematic—Creative
unsystematic—Reactive
untraditional—Creative
untrustworthy—Conceal
untruthful—Conceal
unused—Stay
unusual—Creative
unveil—Reveal
unwavering—Act
unwillingness—Reject
unwind—Creative
unwind—Reactive
unwind—semiconscious
unwind—subconscious
unworried—Accept
unyielding—Reactive
unyielding—Reject
unyielding—Stay
upcoming—time
upfront—Reveal
upgrade—Accumulate
upkeep—Preserve
uprising—Collective
urgent—time
utensils—Accumulate
utensils—Dispose

V – KEYWORDS

vacate—Retreat
vacation—Wait
valid—rational thinking
validate—interaction
validity—Collective
validity—Objective
validity test—Objective
valour—Act
value—matter
vanguard—Advance
vanish—Retreat
variables—Collective
variables—Objective
variables—rational thinking
vehicles—Accumulate
vehicles—Dispose
vehicles—matter
vehicles—Preserve
venture—Prepare
verbal—interaction
verdict—Collective
verify—Collective
verify—Objective
verify—rational thinking
vertical thinking—conventional thinking
vertical thinking—nemonik thinking
veto—Reject
victory—winning
vigilant—Collective
vigilant—conscious
vigilant—Objective
vigilant—perception
vigilant—rational thinking
vigilant—Reactive
villain—Collective

violence—Collective
virtuoso—Reactive
virtuoso—subconscious
vision—Prepare
visionary—Creative
visual—reality
visual sense—perception
volition—mind
volition—Reactive
volume—matter

W – KEYWORDS

wages—Accumulate
wait—nemonik
wait—nemonik thinking
wait—reality
wait—space
wait—Wait
wakeful—Collective
wakeful—conscious
wakeful—Objective
wane—Retreat
war—Collective
war—conventional thinking
war—winning
warden—Preserve
warehouse—Preserve
warfare—winning
warn—Reveal
wary—Reject
wary—Wait
waste—Dispose
watch—perception
watchful—conscious
watching—conscious
watchman—Preserve
wavering—Wait
way of least resistance—Collective
way of least resistance—Objective
way of least resistance—rational thinking
way of least resistance—Reactive
wealth—Accumulate
wealth—Dispose
wealth—matter
wealth—Preserve
weight—matter
wetware—mind

what—matter
when—time
where—space
whistle-blower,—Reveal
white lie—Conceal
width—matter
will—mind
will—Reactive
willing—Accept
willpower—conscious
willpower—Reactive
win-lose—Conceal
win-lose strategies—conventional thinking
win-lose strategies—winning
winning—conventional thinking
winning—nemonik thinking
win-win—Reveal
win-win strategies—nemonik thinking
win-win strategies—success
wipe-out—Dispose
wisdom—affectorial thinking
wisdom—Reactive
wise—nemonik thinking
wise—Preserve
wish—mind
withdraw,—Retreat
wither—Retreat
wizard—Reactive
wizard—subconscious
words—interaction
workforce—Accumulate
workforce—Dispose
workforce—matter
workforce—Preserve
write—projection
write—Reveal
written—Collective

wunderkind—Reactive
wunderkind—subconscious

Y – KEYWORDS

yesterday—time
yield—Accumulate
yielding—Accept

Z – KEYWORDS

zone—affectorial thinking
zone—Creative
zone—Reactive
zone—semiconscious
zone—subconscious

APPENDICES

BIBLIOGRAPHY

Schade, A. (2015). bioPAD: Nemonik Thinking (PowerPoint). Dunedin: nemonik-thinking.org.

Schade, A. (2016). *Global Warming is the Solution.* nemonik-thinking.org.

Schade, A. (2016). *Glossary Nemonik Thinking.* nemonik-thinking.org.

Schade, A. (2016). *Think Smarter with Nemonik Thinking.* nemonik-thinking.org.

Schade, A. (planned 2017). *Lao Zi's Dao De Jing.* nemonik-thinking.org.

Schade, A. (planned 2017). *Sun Zi's The Art of War.* nemonik-thinking.org.

Schade, A. (planned 2017). *The Unreal Reality.* nemonik-thinking.org.

Download free eBooks and videos
@ nemonik-thinking.org

ABSTRACTS OTHER BOOKS

THINK SMARTER...

Think Smarter with Nemonik Thinking (Schade, 2016). This is
the operating manual for your mind that you should have re-
ceived at birth. Nemonik thinking is a smarter way of thinking that aims to maximize your success by evaluating seventeen nemoniks, which are memorized keywords describing all
the perceived aspects of your mind, reality, and their interaction. Success is obtaining what you seek and escaping what
you suffer. Therefore, it is goal oriented. To maximize your
success, nemonik thinking mobilizes your hidden genius, accelerates your thinking, improves your memory, reveals opportunities and threats, creates questions and ideas, and reduces your stress levels. It is like playing a musical keyboard
with seventeen keys producing an infinite repertoire of smart
strategies. Nemonik thinking is unique because it is the first
exhaustive and transferable way of thinking. Comparisons
with Sir Richard Branson's way of thinking show that it is
extremely productive. Unfortunately, the educational system
conditions students still with pass-fail grades to win. Winning
is defeating opponents in competition. Therefore, it is conflict oriented. The compulsion to win inhibits the truth and,
therefore, fosters the corrupted way of conventional thinking.
Conventional thinking creates the malignant cognitive virus
CS7. In turn, that virus consolidates conventional thinking
with cognitive dissonance and groupthink. Conventional
thinking is time consuming. Hence, the less time you have,
the greater the necessity to study nemonik thinking. You
might be the best thinker in the world, but only nemonik
thinking could make you the smartest thinker you can be.

Download a free eBook version
@ nemonik-thinking.org

GLOSSARY...

Glossary of Nemonik Thinking (Schade 2016). Nemonik think-ing is a competitive advantage because it mobilizes your hid-den genius, accelerates your thinking, improves your memory, prevents blind-spots, and reveals opportunities, while its con-stant preparedness reduces stress levels. Definitions associat-ed with the mind and reality are inherently hypothetical, fuzzy, and intertwined. Nevertheless, to improve our under-standing of the way we think, we have to identify, differenti-ate, and define those components. Therefore, this glossary provides descriptions for the concepts associated with nemonik thinking. To become skilled in nemonik thinking, it is recommended to study—*Think Smarter with Nemonik Think-ing (Schade, 2016).*

Download a free eBook version
@ nemonik-thinking.org

GLOBAL WARMING...

Global Warming is the Solution (Schade 2016). This study presents a bilateral synthesis of artificial global warming and natural global cooling. Mainstream climatology lacks scientific integrity and statistical methodology. Peer review is changed into peer pressure and objectors are labelled *"Deniers"*. Proper statistical analyses are replaced by graphs and non-causal correlation analyses that are based on the last 166 years, while 420,000 years of Antarctic data are mainly discarded. Furthermore, climatology ignores that 400 ppm of CO_2 predicts a global temperature of 11.5 °C, rather than the current 1.3 °C. It focuses on artificial global warming and overlooks the threat of natural global cooling. It also ignores the solar expert Professor Zharkova, who predicts a mini ice-age by 2030, which is likely to turn global warming into global cooling. The current study compared the Antarctic temperatures during the last 10,000 years (baseline 0.00 °C) with the global temperature of 1.3 °C. This common definition of global warming failed to reach statistical significance. However, the Antarctic temperatures during the last 420.000 years support the notion that we live in a glacial period of -8.9 °C, rather than in an interglacial period of 0.00 °C. In that case, the artificial global warming would be 10.2 °C, rather than 1.3 °C. This alternative definition of global warming is statistically significant. Furthermore, it is supported by the current CO_2 level of 400 ppm and the significant duration and stability of the current interglacial. Consequently, decreasing the CO_2 level could cause a global disaster threatening the survival of humanity. The increased thermal range and the precarious balance between artificial global warming and natural global cooling could also explain the current climatological instability.

Download a free eBook version
@ nemonik-thinking.org

LAO ZI'S DAO DE JING

Lao Zi's Dao De Jing—The Way (Schade, planned 2017). In one
curt sentence, Lao Zi explains the core of his book—Use it to
obtain what you seek and to escape what you suffer. His in-
spirational guideline introduces the sophisticated yet simple
principle of Dao. This principle explains the Universe, the
meaning of life, and our place in nature. For more than two
and a half thousand years, *Dao De Jing* has been shrouded in
mystery. Many scholars have studied that intriguing manu-
script by peeling away layer after layer of meaning to unravel
its cryptic secrets. Nevertheless, this interpretation shows
that *Dao De Jing* preserved its ancient secrets within a prosaic
collection of aphorisms. These mysteries are revealed for the
first time ever in a clearly understandable way, imparting for-
gotten knowledge about the Universe and the art of living.
To become skilled in nemonik thinking, it is recommended to
study—*Think Smarter with Nemonik Thinking (Schade, 2016).*

Download a free eBook version
@ nemonik-thinking.org

SUN ZI'S THE ART OF WAR

Sun Zi's Bin Fa—The Art of War (Schade, planned 2017). Sun Zi (~6th cent. BC) was a Chinese warrior-philosopher who wrote the military classic *Bing Fa* or *The Art of War.* Although his book is about war, his strategies apply to every facet of daily life. Sun Zi deals with the art of positioning yourself in space, matter, and time. He addresses the questions raised by nemonik thinking of where, what, and when to advance, stay, retreat, accumulate, preserve, dispose, act, wait, prepare, accept, reject, reveal, and conceal. Think smarter and incorporate Sun Zi's strategies in your thinking. To become skilled in nemonik thinking, it is recommended to study—*Think Smarter with Nemonik Thinking (Schade, 2016).*

Download a free eBook version
@ nemonik-thinking.org

COVER DESIGN

The mirror images on the front and back of the cover illustrate the intentional emptiness of this manual. This manual is referred to as *empty* because nemonik thinking is not fostering or inhibiting any cult, doctrine, dogma, ideology, or religion. Nemonik thinking generates questions and ideas, rather than answers or opinions. Responses to those questions and ideas depend on the actual situation and the belief system of the thinker. Nemonik thinking is a neutral mental skill that activates your thinking. It is about how to think, rather than what to believe. Seeing a deeper meaning in it is a clear misunderstanding concerning the essence of nemonik thinking.

DECLARATION OF INDEPENDENCE

I, Dr Auke Schade, declare that this study and the development of nemonik thinking were funded by private resources. No part of this study, or the development of nemonik thinking, was supported, financially or otherwise, by any third party including individuals, stakeholders, charities, commercial, academic, political, ideological, military, religious, and secret organizations. Consequently, I am an independent researcher and do not have to please anyone.

The main global problems are symptoms of humanity's dramatically failing way of thinking. Although a huge and immediate threat, climate change is only one of the many symptoms. Seen the lethargic response of leaders to global warming, it would be unwise to rely on the global establishment for adequate action. Turning the tide in time will require huge sacrifices and resources. Therefore, support from any individual or organisation will be welcomed, as long as it will not comprise my academic integrity.

Now, after the completion of this study and the development of nemonik thinking, I feel even free to approach the oil and coal industries for funding. Confirmation of the bilateral climate-change hypothesis would transform them from villains into heroes. Their industrial CO_2 might save us from living on a frozen planet.

Donations Welcome!

WEBSITE

It is the aim of the website *nemonik-thinking.org* to provide interactive on-line information about nemonik thinking. This includes discussions, books, blog, videos, exercises, updates, activities, web links, and tests. Join the nemonik thinkers and receive the latest updates. It is a work in progress. Check it out and have your say! I look forward to your feedback at:

nemonik-thinking.org